Shine Brighter

The High Performer's Guide to Purpose, Presence, and Peak Living

LAURA KING

burning soul press

Paperback ISBN: 978-1-964924-18-2

Hardcover ISBN: 978-1-964924-19-9

eBook ISBN: 978-1-964924-20-5

This book is a work of nonfiction. Some names and identifying details may have been changed to protect privacy.

DEDICATION

To my mother:
Thank you for teaching me the depth of compassion

To my father:
Thank you for teaching me self-discipline and perseverance

To my kids:
For showing me what life is truly about

To Brian:
For loving me so much you made me a better person

To my friends:
For helping me find more fun and giggle a lot

To Lauren:
For believing in me more than I believed in myself

To Theresa:
For being a gift from above

Table of Contents

Preface

I didn't set out to write a book. I set out to get unstuck.

For years, I was living a life that looked good on the outside. I checked all the boxes: career success, a full calendar, a family I adore. But underneath all the productivity and performance, I felt…disconnected. I wasn't *unhappy*. But I also wasn't lit up. I wasn't fully alive.

And that truth, that quiet ache, was something I could no longer ignore.

The invitation came in the form of a breakdown.

"Oh Laura, I am so sorry to share this news with you," the neurofeedback provider began, his words setting off flutters in my stomach. "Not only do you have anxiety off the charts, but your brain waves show you are not finding rest during the day or at night. You also show the brain wave patterns of ADHD."

The diagnosis was a triple threat: anxiety off the charts, no sleep, and ADHD. At that moment, time seemed to freeze. A part of me wasn't surprised—I had felt the weight of these struggles for years—but seeing them confirmed in data felt like a revelation.

Of course you are anxious, Laura. Of course you're not sleeping. And is it really news to you that you have ADHD?

As this kind man—both a neurotherapy provider and a trained therapist—offered me a hug, I melted into his embrace, tears streaming down my face. I barely knew this man, but my rational brain surrendered to my emotions. I had buried so much for so long. I hadn't realized just how deep the pain ran.

Ironically, I hadn't come to the clinic for myself—I had come for my son, seeking treatment for his anxiety and ADHD. But a quiet voice whispered, "Laura, this is your path too." It was an invitation to finally confront the unresolved emotions and trauma I had shoved under the rug for years.

I started this book at the height of my "broken" moment in spring of 2023; today, it's spring of 2025. So much has changed. This book has been my therapy, my reckoning, my path to purpose. And for the first time in my adult life, I am truly at peace. And that's what I want for you: utmost peace. To see that God uses the darkness to reveal the light. What feels like your worst nightmare is often an invitation to something greater than you could ever imagine.

Before we go deeper, some context:

My awakening began in 2018 with a hearing loss diagnosis. It continued in 2019 with a surprise fourth pregnancy. It deepened in 2020, during the pandemic, as I found a new level of faith. And 2023…oh 2023. The year that shook me to my core. It was painful and terrifying and still seems like a total blur because I wasn't fully "here". I was swirling and living from my mind, not rooted at all in the present moment. I was not an enjoyable person to be around and am very disappointed in how I showed up in my relationships and my work. But there was a purpose behind all of it—a much grander purpose than I could have ever imagined.

The depth of the pain I experienced in 2023 is what I feel so many are going through right now. If you've picked up this book, odds are you're going through an awakening process. What is awakening, you might ask?

Awakening is the realization of who you really are: an eternal spirit in a human body. And the "work" of awakening is unlearning the patterns of the world that keep us small.

What kept me small for most of my life was the story I told myself that I wasn't good enough. So instead of being me, fully me, I became the person that others needed me to be. I performed. Performance came in the currency of earning others' approval, getting top grades, making my parents proud, being valued by my bosses, and seeking others' validation. I cared far too long about what others thought of me. I gave my power away to others. That part of me is dying. And it needs to. Because stress through the roof, not sleeping, and always-on anxiety is no way to live.

"Death is a stripping away of all that is not you. The secret of life is to 'die before you die'—and find that there is no death."
— Eckhart Tolle

Yes, there are parts of you—just like there were parts of me— screaming to evolve. Through this process, I've learned our struggles aren't signs of being "broken." They're invitations to a deeper, more authentic life.

I once lived in the dark, believing I was a victim of my circumstances. Now, I live in the light. In the light is where your freedom, joy and abundance are secured. It's all a choice. You get to choose. You can move from surviving to thriving. It starts with a decision: to take full responsibility for your life.

My sincere hope is that over the next several days, weeks, or however long it takes you to get through these pages, you walk away knowing that your future is bright and **our collective future is bright.** Even if the outside world looks quite the opposite. There is a light inside you, inside all of us, waiting to be unleashed.

Shine Brighter is about breaking those barriers. It's about **remembering who you truly are.**

Throughout my 42 years on earth, I've developed an intuitive ability to sense the energy people bring—to see beyond titles and accomplishments into what really matters. 30,000 interviews as an executive recruiter, placing thousands into new jobs, and being the person other people call when they need help "figuring things out" - I have a gift in reading people and reading energy. And guess what? Your energy tells me exactly how much light you're letting in.

I see it when you are holding yourself back. I see it when you lie to yourself. I see it when you hesitate. I know this because I did the same thing. I lied to myself for a very long time, pretending to be happy.

These are the questions I began to ask myself that helped me on my journey, and I advise you to ask yourself right now: Are you *really* happy? Are you doing what lights you up? Are you serving the people you *really* want to serve? Are you experiencing elevated emotions such as joy, vibrancy and aliveness on a daily basis?

These questions reveal the truth. And to find the hero within us, we must step back and see our lives through a new lens. An honest lens.

We are all on a hero's journey—a concept Joseph Campbell popularized, which mirrors our own evolution:

- **Call to Adventure:** You are invited to step into something greater.
- **Mentorship:** You meet guides who help you navigate the unknown.
- **Crossing the Threshold:** You leave the familiar and embrace change.
- **Trials and Tribulations:** You face struggles that test and refine you.
- **Transformation:** You emerge with new wisdom and purpose.
- **Return with the Elixir:** You bring your newfound insight back to the world.

Take a moment, close this book, breathe deeply, and ask yourself: What journey am I on?

For me, the journey has been moving from a striver   always chasing approval—to loving every part of me as I am. Yours might be different. But we all end up at the same place. I just want to help you get there a *little* faster. I am an activator and I'm here to activate you.

Ready?

A little more mojo before we really get into the meaty stuff:

Each of us is born with a unique mission. We are not here to *conform* but to uncover and embrace our true selves. Your unique genius is your gift to the world. It's not selfish to embark on a journey of self-discovery—it's necessary.

A common regret of the dying is: *I wish I'd had the courage to live a life true to myself, not the life others expected of me.*

Let that sink in.

Way too many people have confided in me at the end of their careers that they regret the lives they built. Many of us wouldn't want our children to follow in our footsteps—yet we keep walking the same path. It's time to wake up. The younger generations see our unhappiness. They can tell when we're just going through the motions. So why can't we?

Because honesty with ourselves is hard. Because our brains crave safety and familiarity. Because we've been conditioned to follow patterns that don't serve us. Because we've learned to limit ourselves. We've learned to be fearful.

But here's the truth: You have free will. You get to decide how this goes. And you can always choose again. If you are reading these words, you are incredibly powerful and you can choose a new adventure.

This journey is as much about unlearning as it is about remembering.

I believe in you. I believe in your dreams. I believe there's a life beyond your wildest imagination waiting for you. You just have to surrender to the whispers inside you—the ones nudging you toward truth and light and joy that lead you exactly to these words.

By picking up this book, you've already taken the first step. You're ready.

Now, I want you to pause and reflect on these questions (be honest). Also, sorry not sorry for all the questions. Questions are kind of my jam.

- Are you satisfied with your life? Tolerating or genuinely satisfied?
- How present are you, truly, in your day?
- Are you intentionally creating your life, or just going through the motions?
- If you had a chance to do it all again, would you live/be the same way?

Seriously—grab a journal. Answer them.

Through sharing my story and the lessons I've learned from the thousands of people whose lives I've touched, my hope is that you let go of what no longer serves you, reconnect with who you truly are, and take action on what you desire most.

You are enough, exactly as you are. And as we walk through these pages together, I pray that you see just how powerful you truly are. It's time to break free from what's been holding you back and let your light shine brighter than ever before.

Introduction

There comes a moment in life when the success you've worked so hard for begins to feel… hollow.

You've climbed the ladder, checked the boxes, and proved your worth in a thousand ways. And yet, deep inside, a quiet question persists:

Is this it?

If that question resonates with you — if you've found yourself performing rather than *being*, striving rather than *thriving* — then this book found you for a reason.

This is not about doing more. It's about *becoming more of who you already are.*

It's for the high achiever who's quietly burning out. The caregiver who's lost herself in the roles she plays. The successful professional who feels spiritually off-course, even when everything "looks" right.

This is your invitation to come back home to yourself.

And the journey begins with a powerful, yet simple framework: **The 4 A's—Awareness, Attitude, Action, and Alignment.**

AWARENESS: The Power of Seeing Clearly

Awareness is the gateway to transformation. You can't change what you can't see. This first "A" is about lifting the veil — tuning in to your thoughts, behaviors, and beliefs without judgment.

Neuroscience shows that 95% of our thoughts and behaviors are unconscious, running on autopilot. That means most of us are living out patterns we didn't consciously choose. Awareness interrupts that cycle.

Awareness invites you to notice:
- When you're in "performer mode" vs. authentic presence
- What beliefs are driving your actions (e.g. "I'm only worthy if I achieve")
- Where you feel stuck, drained, or out of sync

ATTITUDE: The Lens You Choose

Once you become aware, the next step is choosing how you relate to what you see. That's your **attitude**.

Mel Robbins, one of my mentors from afar, speaks often about *activation energy* — the moment you choose to shift your mindset before your brain talks you out of it. This "A" is about shifting from self-criticism to self-compassion, from fear to faith, from resistance to curiosity.

Attitude is where we:
- Replace negative self-talk with empowered thinking
- Develop a "ripple mindset" — knowing even small acts of authenticity matter
- Bring gratitude into difficult moments to expand your capacity for growth

Attitude is your inner posture. And it changes everything.

ACTION: Your Energy in Motion

Too many people get stuck in the "awareness" stage — they know what needs to change but struggle to move forward. That's where **Action** comes in.

One of my favorite mantras is 'clarity happens when you're in motion'. You don't need to have everything figured out before you take the first step. What matters is that you take aligned, consistent action — even if it's small.

This section of the book will help you:
- Turn insights into new habits and micro-moves
- Practice "inspired imperfection" — taking action before you feel ready
- Build a bridge between your inner knowing and outer reality

Transformation doesn't happen in thought alone. It lives in action.

ALIGNMENT: The Integration of Self

This final "A" is what brings it all together — it's where your inner world and outer world begin to match. When you're aligned, life feels more fluid. You're not fighting yourself or proving anything. You're living in integrity with who you are.

Brené Brown calls this "living wholeheartedly." It's when you stop hustling for your worth and start *embodying* it.

In this section, you'll explore:
- How to recognize misalignment (it often shows up as anxiety, resentment, or fatigue)
- Ways to recalibrate when you're off course
- How to cultivate spiritual and emotional congruence

Alignment isn't a destination. It's a lifelong practice. And the more aligned you are, the more radiant your impact becomes.

The Role of Reflection, Meditation & Journaling

These three practices are the throughline of this book. Why? Because they help you slow down, go inward, and meet yourself with honesty and compassion.
- **Meditation** helps calm your nervous system and increase self-awareness
- **Journaling** helps organize your thoughts and to connect patterns
- **Reflection** helps integrate insights into action

Science backs this up: meditation rewires the brain for resilience and clarity. Journaling boosts emotional intelligence and immune function. Reflection creates meaning — the root of purpose.

Each chapter will offer opportunities for you to pause, reflect, and go deeper — not just to "read" but to *experience* change in real time.

How to Use This Book

This book is meant to be returned to again and again. Let it be your mirror, your journal companion, your quiet guide.

> We have a special gift for you! Below you'll find the URL for a free companion workbook with all of the exercises from the book so you can print it out and write in the workbook as many times as you need on this process of refinement and growth. www.lauraeking.com/bonus

Pick and choose the practices that resonate with you. Don't feel like you need to take on everything at once. I give you full permission to skip practices that you're not called to do. Do not feel like you need to "do it perfectly." That is a recipe for overwhelm and that's the last thing I want for you.

You can move through it linearly, or jump to the section that calls to you. Pause after the prompts. Write in the margins when you're guided to. Journal when it feels necessary. Come back to certain practices again. Re-read chapters. Re-listen to the audio version. Let repetition become revelation — because as you'll soon discover, *repetition is the mother of skill*.

This isn't a one-time read. It's a *lifetime practice*.

One Final Word Before We Begin

You don't need to do more to be enough. You already are.

This book will remind you of that truth — and show you how to live from it. The real magic isn't in becoming someone new. It's in remembering who you already are and becoming that.

So take a deep breath.

You're not broken. You're not behind. You're not too late.

You're right on time.

PART I

Foundations of Authentic Living

Unlocking Truth

"The more you see yourself as what you'd like to become, and act as if what you want is already there, the more you'll activate those dormant forces that will collaborate to transform your dream into your reality."

– Wayne Dyer

Imagine if everything you believed about yourself—your worth, your identity, your potential—was built on a misconception. What if the foundation of how you measure your value was flawed?

This isn't just a thought experiment. It's a reality for most of us.

From the moment we enter the world, we are conditioned to equate our worth with what we do—our achievements, our careers, our productivity. Society has drilled into us that success is external: the job title, the bank account, the social media following. But what if this entire framework is misguided?

Let me ask you: What if you are more than the things you do?

Take a moment right now. Write down three things that define who you are. Go ahead, I'll wait.

Now, look at your list. How many of those things are tied to what you do—your job, your roles, your responsibilities? If most or all of them are, you're not alone. This is the very illusion we're here to break.

Because unlocking truth is about uncovering what's real beneath the labels, the achievements, the noise. It's about reclaiming your identity—not as the sum of your accomplishments, but as the infinite, worthy, powerful being you were created to be.

Sit with that for a moment. This question challenges our deeply ingrained beliefs and ignites a spark of possibility within us. It strikes at the heart of what's truly blocking our inner light from shining.

My Awakening: The Funeral Exercise

I vividly remember the moment this truth hit me like a lightning bolt. It was 2015, and I was sitting in a conference room when a speaker posed a startling question: "Who here has envisioned their funeral?"

Well, that certainly got my attention.

Over the next 90 minutes, I lost track of time as I listened and began to write my own eulogy. Morbid, you might think? Perhaps. But it forced me to confront a crucial question: What's going to matter when I leave the earth? Will being the #1 biller in my company matter at all? Or will it be about how I treated people, loved people, encouraged them, and stayed true to who I am?

As I wrote feverishly, the truth I had been avoiding, the whisper I'd been too afraid to acknowledge, became crystal clear: I am not what I do. I am so much more.

Here's a glimpse of what I wrote over a decade ago:

"Laura King was known for her zest for life, her love for all humans, and her radiating energy to everyone she met. If you know Laura, then you know she was all about seeing you as you truly are at the soul level. She made you feel seen, heard, and loved. When you were in her presence, you felt unconditional love.

Laura is survived by her husband of 65 years Brian, and their four adult children Miles William, Brody Michael, Charlie Joseph, and Crosby James—and 12 grandchildren. Laura was a beacon of light for her family. She loved sharing her true, authentic self on massive stages all over the world. While she loved impacting massive amounts of lives through energy and connection and experiences all over the world, what she loved most were the intimate, deep conversations with her family and friends.

Being with her children and grandchildren was the light that kept Laura going in her later years. Witnessing a smile or glance from a loved one could change the entire trajectory of the day. Those were the moments Laura lived for. She always found a way to "bring the joy" to everyday moments—from mundane tasks like doing the dishes to dancing in public (often embarrassing her boys) to family vacations—she made sure she enjoyed life with curiosity and the playlike nature of a child.

Early in her career, Laura set the example of the integration that could exist for purpose-driven leaders to model congruence in work, health, family, spirituality, fitness, and relationships. Laura learned and modeled aligning her personal and professional world in her 30s and felt compelled to pay it forward and teach these strategies to others in her 40s and beyond.

Laura followed an untraditional path in her career. She started and helped grow many businesses, gave thousands of people jobs, and traveled the world spreading messages of hope, faith, and perseverance. Laura inspired millions to wake up to the reality that you create your own reality and shine the brightest when you stop living someone else's version of you and step into your own weird, quirky, authentic self. We are all here to support and love one another, and we are all here to heal. Laura defined success as finding the truest, highest expression of yourself as a human being and then being that in the service of others. She also loved teaching fitness classes well into her 80s.

Above all, Laura was committed to helping more people wake up to their lives and shine brighter. Living a life on purpose. Living intentionally. This life is really not about you at all; it's about the collective. Love for all. When you really get that, you win."

And as I wrote, the truth became clearer and clearer. My legacy, my impact, my very essence had nothing to do with my job title or my accomplishments. It had everything to do with who I am, how I love, and a life filled with service.

This exercise was a wake-up call, forcing me to confront the truth about being versus doing. But then I quickly got swallowed up by "real life," or, that is the story I told myself. I had a family to support, and I was the breadwinner, so I better get to work. All this went on the backburner for years.

Fast forward to the fall of 2023—perhaps the darkest period of my adult life. In spring of that year, I had received devastating news that blindsided me. As I shared in the introduction, what began as seeking help for my son led to my own diagnosis: severe anxiety, chronic sleep disruption, and ADHD.

That triple diagnosis sent me into a tailspin. I had spent years guiding others toward their light while my own was dimming. I had isolated myself from family and friends, convinced I needed to handle my struggles alone. I was drowning in my own suffering, not taking any of the advice I so freely gave to others.

One afternoon while organizing my office, I stumbled upon that obituary I'd written years before. Reading those words while sitting in my pain was a moment of stark clarity. The woman described in those pages—joyful, present, loving, aligned—felt like a stranger to me now. I had to face the truth: I was nowhere near being that person. The gap between who I aspired to be and who I had become was heartbreaking.

I realized I had fallen into a victim mindset. Dr. Steve Maraboli, behavioral scientist and author of *Unapologetically You*, explains this mindset perfectly: "The victim mindset dilutes the human potential. By not accepting personal responsibility for our circumstances, we greatly reduce our power to change them."[7] I had become the victim of my circumstances rather than the creator of my experience.

The path to healing wasn't easy, but it was clear. I needed to practice what I preached. I committed to a combination of counseling, neurofeedback therapy, and the very practices I outline in this book. Neurofeedback—a growing therapeutic approach that trains brainwave patterns through real-time feedback—helped rewire my anxious brain. Sessions twice weekly for several months taught my brain to find calm patterns again. It's the same technique now used by elite athletes to optimize performance and focus, but for me, it was a lifeline back to mental wellness.

You don't need neurofeedback to rewire your brain. You can rewire your brain through consistent meditation that combines intense focus with elevated emotions, breaking old neural patterns while creating new ones, along with visualization techniques, affirmations, and coherent breathing that synchronize your heart and brain. The key is repetition and emotional engagement – when you pair a clear intention with a genuine elevated emotion daily, you create new neural pathways that eventually become your default state of being. In just two pages, I'll give you a step by step process for meditation whether you are an avid or new practitioner.

In summary, the most powerful shift for me, and what I urge you to consider, is this one simple choice: to stop viewing myself as broken and to reclaim responsibility for my life and happiness. I chose to step back into the light, to reconnect with who I am beyond my struggles, my diagnoses, and my achievements.

The Performance Trap

We're trained to be performance-driven from an early age. Think back to your first sports game, grade-school report cards, or that promotion you were eyeing. We're entangled in a world where doing equates to being, a world that declares, "If you're not doing/accomplishing/striving, you're not valuable."

But what if the truth is entirely different? What if who you are, at your core, is so much more than what you do? What if your value lies not in your accomplishments but in your very existence?

Let me share a personal story that illustrates this point. In 2016, my marriage was suffering, I wasn't present for my kids, and I had become obsessed with being the best marketing recruiter in the Twin Cities. I lost sight of what was truly important: those I love, those right in front of me—my husband and my little boys. And myself. I was completely out of alignment. Yes, I had written my eulogy and then forgot about living into that person.

I was defining myself solely by my job title and my accomplishments. "Hi, I'm Laura, and I'm an Executive Recruiter," I'd say at networking events, as if that summed up my entire being. But that's not who I am. That's just what I do.

But who am I beyond that?

FEATURED PRACTICE:
The Identity Introduction

Introduce yourself to an imaginary person, but you're not allowed to mention what you do for a living or any of your accomplishments. How would you describe yourself? What aspects of your character, your passions, your values would you share?

> This simple yet profound exercise reveals what truly matters to you beyond your professional identity. Research by Dr. Brené Brown shows that people who can separate their self-worth from their achievements demonstrate greater resilience in the face of failure and setbacks.[1]

We often forget this truth in the hustle of daily life: we are not what we do. We are who we are—and that's so much more than jobs, titles, or accomplishments.

Now, let's take this idea even deeper. Stay with me here—have you ever considered that a human body weighs the same both alive and dead? The difference is something intangible, weightless. It's your spirit, your essence—the "you" that is more than just a body. The part that has no physical weight but carries immense power, purpose, and energy.

And yet, we spend so much of our lives in relentless pursuit of doing, achieving, proving. But what if real fulfillment isn't found in doing at all? What if it's found in simply being? Imagine allowing yourself to feel complete and worthy, not because of what you've done, but because of who you are—right here, right now. This is freedom. This is connection to your eternal spirit. This is how we truly connect to God, or a higher power, or the Universe (you pick the one you resonate with the most).

As a parent, I've experienced the deep truth of this. Those moments when your child needs comfort, and all they really need is for you to be there—your presence is enough. Your eyes meet theirs, and in that unspoken exchange, they feel safe, loved, and understood. What did you really do? Nothing. You were just there. And that made all the difference.

> **Reflection Moment:** When was the last time your presence alone—not your advice, not your actions, just your being there—made a difference to someone? How did that feel compared to achievement-based validation?

I challenge you to practice presence in your daily life. The next time you're with a loved one, put away distractions. Don't try to fix, solve, or advise—just be there, fully present. Notice how it feels for both of you.

Living in alignment with your truth means recognizing your infinite worth—independent of achievements or expectations. For me, that always points back to God. My faith fuels my actions, reminding me daily: I am a child of God. I am eternal. I am here to bless, to be a light, to hold space for others. When I live from this truth, I move forward with confidence, knowing I'm on the right path.

Remember old Laura—the one stressed and anxious all the time? That Laura is a girl I don't recognize anymore. But when old parts of me come up (because they still do from time to time), I choose to step into light and love. In those moments, I release everything that isn't truly me—shame, guilt, unworthiness. I returned to the version of myself that had always been there, the childlike essence of who I really am: innocent and pure.

Declare who you are and believe it. Whatever follows "I am" becomes your reality.

What truth will you choose to unlock?

The Power of Meditation: Coming Home to Yourself

Let's start with a simple meditation.

I know, you might be rolling your eyes—but hear me out. Meditation has been a powerful tool in my journey. It helps quiet the mind, opens the heart, and makes space for divine guidance. It softens resistance, allowing life to work through us rather than against us.

When we're open, we become present. And in presence, we experience life more fully. We stop chasing, start accepting, and surrender to something greater.

FEATURED PRACTICE: One-Minute Presence Meditation

1. Sit comfortably and close your eyes.
2. Take three deep breaths, focusing on the air entering and leaving your body.
3. For one minute, observe your thoughts without judgment. Let them pass like clouds in the sky.
4. Open your eyes. How do you feel?

This brief practice connects you to your true self, beyond the constant "doing." Neuroscience research shows that even short meditation sessions can reduce activity in the brain's default mode network, which is responsible for self-referential thoughts and mind-wandering.[2]

A Few Meditation Myths—Busted

Myth: You won't have thoughts.

Truth: Actually, you will. Sometimes they'll race, and you'll think you're doing it wrong (you're not). Other times, things will slow down, and you'll feel deeply guided.

Myth: There's a right way to meditate.

Truth: Nope. There's only your way. Any method that helps you connect with your essence is the right one. You can't mess this up—just keep showing up.

Myth: Something big always happens.

Truth: Not necessarily. Each session is unique. What matters isn't just the experience itself but how it impacts your daily life— how it helps you stay grounded in your truth amidst the noise.

The 4 A's: A Framework for Alignment

Throughout each chapter, I'll guide you through a powerful approach I call the 4 A's Framework—Awareness, Attitude, Action, and Alignment. This proven system has transformed my life and countless others by helping us reconnect with who we truly are beyond our achievements. It's the foundation for the journey we'll take together.

I write from a place of deep practice, not theory. Everything I share comes from hundreds of hours studying personal development through online trainings, in-person seminars, and countless books—but more importantly, from applying these principles in my own life and guiding others through their transformations. The ultimate test isn't knowledge; it's implementation. And I've been in the trenches, doing this work myself, living these principles even when it was hardest to do so.

To help you unlock your truth and embrace who you are beyond achievements, let's explore each component of the 4 A's Framework in depth.

1. Awareness

Awareness is recognizing the thoughts and beliefs that shape your identity. This can be uncomfortable—seeing where you've been limiting yourself. But it's also empowering. Once you see it, you can change it.

The journey to truth begins with becoming aware of the stories you've been telling yourself. These stories often come from childhood, society, or even well-meaning loved ones. But they may not reflect your authentic self.

Awareness is like turning on a light in a dark room. Suddenly, you can see what's actually there, not just what you imagined. You notice patterns in your thinking: "I'm only valuable when I'm productive" or "My worth depends on others' approval." Recognizing these patterns is the first step to changing them.

Optional Exercises:

- Track how often you define yourself by what you do in a day. You might be surprised.
- Set aside five minutes daily to reflect: Are you feeling valued for who you are or just for what you do?

2. Attitude

Shifting your perspective changes everything. Instead of judging yourself, approach your journey with curiosity. Attitude is about how you relate to what you discover about yourself—with criticism or compassion.

Your attitude creates your experience. When you view yourself through the lens of curiosity rather than judgment, you open the door to transformation. Instead of thinking, "I'm so stuck in these patterns," try, "I'm learning about these patterns so I can grow beyond them."

Psychology professor Carol Dweck's research on mindset shows that people who believe they can develop their abilities (a growth mindset) achieve more than those who believe their talents are fixed traits.[3] This applies to your relationship with yourself as well.

Optional Exercises:

- Enjoy a cup of coffee without multitasking.
- Sit in a park and just observe—no phone, no agenda.
- Give yourself permission to be without the pressure to do.

3. Action

Change happens when you make choices aligned with your true self. Every action reinforces new beliefs, rewiring your brain to operate from your soul instead of your ego.

Awareness and attitude prepare the ground, but action plants the seeds of transformation. This doesn't mean adding more to your to-do list. Often, it means doing less but with greater intention and presence.

Actions that align with your essence might look counterintuitive in our productivity-obsessed culture. Taking time to rest, to play, to simply be—these can be the most powerful actions for reclaiming your identity beyond achievements.

Optional Exercises:

- Implement a daily practice that connects you to your core—meditation, journaling, nature walks.
- Do something purely for joy, with no goal attached.
- Take intentional breaks from productivity to reconnect with yourself.

4. Alignment

When your thoughts, feelings, and actions align with your essence, life flows. Alignment isn't a destination—it's an ongoing practice of tuning in, adjusting, and staying true to yourself.

When you live in alignment, you start attracting people, experiences, and opportunities that resonate with your truth. Challenges still arise, but you meet them with resilience and grace. You stop chasing external validation because you know your worth is unshakable.

Alignment feels like coming home to yourself. There's an ease, a rightness to your days. You're not fighting against your nature or forcing yourself into roles that don't fit. You're living authentically, from the inside out.

Optional Exercises:

- Check in with yourself: Are your daily actions aligned with who you truly are?
- Find harmony between "doing" and "being."
- Dedicate time weekly to activities that align with your values.

From Theory to Transformation: Real Stories of Change

These principles aren't just theoretical—they transform real lives. Let me tell you about my client, Terry (name changed to protect my coaching client's confidentiality).

When Terry first came to me, he was drowning in a sea of negative thoughts about his career and the overall trajectory of his life. As a corporate executive working 60+ hours weekly, he felt disconnected from his family and himself. "I'm successful on paper," he told me in our first session, "but I feel like a complete failure as a father and husband. I don't even know who I am anymore beyond my job title."

Terry committed to the 4 A's process. First, through awareness exercises, he recognized how deeply he had tied his worth to his professional achievements and external validation. His attitude shifted as he practiced self-compassion rather than harsh self-judgment. Then came action—he began scheduling non-negotiable family time, started a morning meditation practice, and set boundaries at work.

The alignment came gradually but powerfully. Within six months, Terry had not only reconnected with his family but had found the courage to launch the consulting practice he'd dreamed of for years. Today, he works fewer hours while making a bigger impact, exercises regularly, and most importantly, shows up as the present father and husband he always wanted to be.

"The framework didn't just change what I do," Terry told me recently. "It changed who I am and how I see myself. For the first time, I'm proud of who I am, not just what I've accomplished."

I live for these transformations. They remind me that when we reconnect with our true essence—when we value being over doing—everything changes. Our relationships deepen. Our work becomes more meaningful. Our presence in the world becomes a gift rather than a performance.

Remember: You're not just a human doing—you're a human being. The power to transform your life isn't in achieving more; it's in embracing who you already are.

When you live from this truth, everything shifts. You stop proving and start being. You stop chasing and start radiating. You no longer seek validation.

The journey I've shared with you—from writing my eulogy, to losing my way, to finding myself again through the darkness of 2023—is evidence that this transformation is possible for anyone. We all face moments when we must choose: Will we remain victims of our circumstances, or will we become creators of our experience?

As Dr. Edith Eger, Holocaust survivor and renowned psychologist, writes in her book *The Choice*: "We cannot choose to have a life free of hurt. But we can choose to be free, to escape the past, no matter what befalls us, and to embrace the possible."[8]

The ultimate choice is yours. You can realize that you are inherently worthy simply because you exist, or you can choose to sit in a victim mindset that says your worth depends on what happens to you or what you accomplish. It really is a choice—perhaps the most important one you'll ever make.

Key Takeaways:

- Your worth is inherent and exists independent of your achievements or productivity
- Meditation and presence practices help quiet the "doing" mind and connect with your essence
- Small, intentional shifts in daily life can transform your relationship with yourself
- True fulfillment comes from being who you are, not from what you achieve
- The victim mindset gives away your power; the creator mindset reclaims it
- Healing is possible—through professional support, inner work, and conscious choice

Expert Insights on Being vs. Doing

"We are human beings, not human doings. Don't equate your self-worth with how well you do things in life. You aren't what you do. If you are what you do, then when you don't...you aren't." — Dr. Wayne Dyer, whose research and writings on self-actualization have helped millions reconnect with their authentic selves.[4]

"In a society that relentlessly promotes avarice and excess as the good life, a person happy doing his own work is usually considered an eccentric, if not a subversive." — Bill Watterson, creator of Calvin and Hobbes, who famously walked away from commercial success to preserve his artistic integrity.[5]

"Being must be felt. It can't be thought." — Eckhart Tolle, whose work on presence and consciousness has transformed our understanding of human awareness and fulfillment.[6]

"The victim mindset dilutes the human potential. By not accepting personal responsibility for our circumstances, we greatly reduce our power to change them." — Dr. Steve Maraboli, behavioral scientist and author of *Unapologetically You*, who studies the psychology of human potential and self-empowerment.[7]

Your Turn: Reflective Free Writing

Take a few minutes now to explore your own relationship with being versus doing. Find a quiet space, set a timer for 10 minutes, and write continuously without editing or judging what comes up. You might consider these prompts:

Free Writing Prompts:

- If I weren't defined by my job, accomplishments, or roles, who would I be?
- How might my relationships change if I valued presence over productivity?
- If I wrote my own eulogy today, what would I want it to say about who I was, not just what I did?

Unlocking Your Worthiness

"The reward for conformity is that everyone likes you but yourself."

– Rita Mae Brown

Have you ever felt like you're not enough? Like no matter what you do, no matter how hard you try, you just can't seem to measure up to some invisible standard of worthiness? If so, you're not alone. This feeling of unworthiness is an epidemic in our society, a silent struggle that so many of us face every day.

But what if I told you that this feeling of unworthiness is actually a gateway, a doorway to discovering the incredible light that resides within you? What if, by facing and embracing your unworthiness, you could unlock a level of self-love, self-acceptance, and self-empowerment beyond your wildest dreams?

It's true. The path to your inner light, to your true power and potential, lies not in denying or overcoming your unworthiness, but in deeply and completely accepting it.

From the moment we're born, we're bombarded with messages about what it means to be worthy. We're told we need to look a certain way, behave a certain way, and achieve certain things to be acceptable, lovable, and valuable. We internalize these messages, creating a set of conditions for our worthiness that we strive to meet.

But here's the problem: these conditions are always changing. The goalposts are always moving. No matter how much we achieve, no matter how perfect we try to be, there's always something more we could be doing, something we need to improve. It's an unwinnable game.

And so, we live our lives feeling perpetually unworthy, striving and struggling and pushing ourselves to exhaustion in an attempt to prove our value. We wear masks and play roles, hiding our true selves for fear that if anyone saw who we really are, they would deem us unworthy.

But in doing so, we cut ourselves off from our inner light. We dim our own radiance, believing it to be inadequate. We settle for a life of going through the motions, never truly alive, never truly lit up from within.

It doesn't have to be this way.

Unworthiness as a Messenger

Your unworthiness, the very thing you've been trying to hide from and overcome, is actually the key to your liberation. It's the buried treasure, the hidden gem that, when excavated and polished, reveals the stunning brilliance of your being.

How? By showing you where you've been disconnected from your truth. By illuminating the ways in which you've been living out of alignment with your authentic self. By bringing to light the stories, the beliefs, the patterns that have been keeping you small.

It might show up as a tight feeling in your chest when you're about to speak up in a meeting, a sign that you're afraid of being seen and heard. It might show up as a sinking sensation in your stomach when you compare yourself to others, a signal that you're measuring your worth based on external factors. It might appear as a critical voice in your head, telling you all the ways you're falling short, a clue that you're holding yourself to impossible standards.

> **Reflection Moment:** When do you feel most unworthy? Notice where you feel it in your body. What message might this feeling be trying to convey?

Feeling accepted as I am has been a lifelong struggle. My sense of unworthiness traces back to 7th and 8th grade when I was bullied—eating lunch in the bathroom alone, too afraid to face the girls who had once been my friends. Overnight, they decided I wasn't "cool" enough. They wrote a list—25 Reasons We Hate Laura—and taped the list on my locker for everyone to see. Even my best friend turned against me. I wasn't confident. I just wanted to disappear. This trauma left a lasting impression on me for decades. I feared going to school. I had no friends.

Even now, walking into a room full of women can trigger those old wounds. Just when I think I've healed, something new surfaces, revealing where there's still work to do. The other day, I convinced myself that someone I admired didn't like me. Was it true? I had no idea. But my mind ran with the story, desperate for her approval. Then I caught myself—this wasn't 42-year-old Laura reacting. This was 13-year-old Laura, still seeking validation. She's still in there doubting herself, not confident and unsure. Wild, right? Because I sure look confident from the outside. But inside, those feelings of unworthiness still pop up and I have to learn to discern what's truth vs. what the story I am telling myself.

It's wild how our minds can spin stories from thin air, turning fleeting thoughts into elaborate narratives. The good news? We don't have to believe them. It starts with awareness—catching the story before it consumes us and shifting from the mind into the heart.

The Universal Nature of Unworthiness

No one has ever existed exactly like you. You are one of a kind. A big part of my purpose in my work is helping others see their brilliance. I speak truth into people every day, reminding them of their uniqueness. I am open about my struggles and offer a safe space for them to share. In return, I'm never surprised when many share their insecurities with me.

Just the other day, a CEO of a publicly traded company confided in me about her self-doubt. Years ago, that would have shocked me. Now, I expect it. When I'm at peace with who I am and offer a loving presence, people open up—daily. And honestly? It's one of my favorite things to see their realness shine through.

We all have insecurities. Some people share them; others hide them. But believe me—the ones who seem to have it all together are often struggling just as much as you are. I know because I have the data points. Thousands of conversations with professionals from almost two decades in executive search confirm this. So please know you are not alone. Not even for a second. Part of embracing our worth is realizing we're more alike than different. We are united in our humanity. The sooner we're honest with ourselves, the more grace we can extend to others.

Whatever form it takes, your feeling of unworthiness is not a problem to be solved, but a message to be deciphered. It's an invitation to go deeper, to get curious, to explore the uncharted territories of your inner landscape.

The 4 A's Framework for Unlocking Worthiness

The journey of reclaiming your worth can be guided by what I call the 4 A's Framework: Awareness, Attitude, Action, and Alignment. This simple yet powerful approach has transformed my life and countless others I've worked with.

1. Awareness: Seeing the Truth

As you start to shine the light of your awareness on the dark corners of unworthiness, something extraordinary happens.

You start to see that unworthiness is not your true identity. It's just a story, a narrative you've been telling yourself based on a lifetime of conditioning.

One powerful tool for cultivating awareness is mindfulness. By learning to be present in the moment, to observe your thoughts and emotions without judgment, you start to create space between yourself and your unworthiness. You start to see that these thoughts are not who you are, they're just habits of mind.

Another key aspect of awareness is self-reflection. Taking time each day to journal, meditate, and ask yourself deeper questions can help you uncover the roots of your unworthiness. You might start to see how these patterns originated in childhood and how society and culture have reinforced them.

You begin to understand that your worth is not something that needs to be earned or proven. It's inherent, intrinsic, unconditional. It's the very essence of your being, the core of who you are.

> **Try This:** Stand in front of a mirror and look into your own eyes. Say out loud, "I am worthy, just as I am." Notice any resistance that comes up. That resistance is not the truth—it's the old story trying to maintain its grip. Keep repeating the phrase, allowing yourself to feel the truth of it more deeply each time.

2. Attitude: Embracing Self-Compassion

As this realization dawns, as you start to connect with the innate worthiness that has always been there, your light begins to shine brighter. You start to stand taller, speak more clearly, live more boldly. You start to make choices and take actions that align with your truth, rather than with your fears.

Cultivating a positive attitude doesn't mean ignoring or suppressing negative feelings. It means focusing on the potential for growth and learning in every experience. It means adopting a mindset of self-compassion and treating yourself with the same kindness and understanding you would offer a dear friend or a child.

FEATURED PRACTICE:
The Self-Compassion Pause

When feelings of unworthiness arise, try this powerful three-step practice:

1. **Place a hand on your heart** and feel its warmth and gentle pressure
2. **Acknowledge your struggle** with kind words: "This is difficult right now. I'm feeling that old unworthiness."
3. **Offer yourself compassion**: "I see you. I hear you. I'm here with you. This feeling is human, and I'm not alone in experiencing it."

Practice this pause whenever your inner critic becomes loud. Research by Dr. Kristin Neff, a leading expert on self-compassion, shows this practice actually changes your neurochemistry, reducing cortisol (stress hormone) and increasing oxytocin and opiates (feel-good hormones)[1].

This simple act of turning towards your pain with gentleness, of offering yourself the compassion you so freely give to others, can be revolutionary. It can start to soften the hard edges of your unworthiness, to melt the shame and self-judgment that lay there, hidden in places you've never allowed yourself to see.

Positive affirmations are another powerful way to shift your attitude. Each morning, look in the mirror and say, "I am worthy of love and respect, just as I am." Even if you don't believe it at first, consistent practice can gradually reshape your attitude toward yourself.

3. Action: Living Your Worth

This is a journey of coming home to yourself, of reclaiming the parts of you that you've disowned and denied. It's a journey of integrating your shadow, light, humanity, and divinity. And it's a journey that only you can take. You are the only one who can do this work for you. No external validation, no achievement or accolade, no outside force, can give you the sense of worthiness that you seek. It's an inside job, a solo adventure into the depths of your being.

One essential action is setting boundaries. When you're operating from a place of unworthiness, you often say yes to things that don't serve you, that drain your energy and your joy. Learning to say no, to put your own needs first, is a radical act of self-worth.

Another important action is self-care. This means making your physical, emotional, and spiritual well-being a priority. It means nourishing yourself with healthy food, regular movement, and sufficient rest. It means taking time for activities that bring you joy and replenish your energy. Self-care also means surrounding yourself with people and environments that reflect your worthiness back to you. It means seeking out relationships and communities where you feel seen, heard, and valued for who you are. It means letting go of situations and dynamics that diminish or deplete you.

A powerful practice for taking action is gratitude. When you're in the throes of unworthiness, it can be hard to see the good in your life, to recognize the blessings that surround you. But by intentionally cultivating gratitude, by training your mind to look for what's working rather than what's lacking, you start to shift your perspective.

> **Try This:** Each night before bed, write down three things you're grateful for. They can be big or small—the warmth of the sun on your face, a kind word from a friend, the taste of your morning coffee. As you write, really let yourself feel the gratitude in your body. Notice how this practice begins to shift your focus from what's lacking to what's abundant in your life.

You begin to see that even in the midst of your struggles, there is so much to be thankful for. The air in your lungs, the beat of your heart, the people who love you, the beauty of a sunset or a child's laugh. And as you focus on these things, as you fill your heart with appreciation, your sense of worthiness grows. This really began to click for me as I entered 2025 with a profound sense of gratitude and reverence for my life, my husband, and my four boys.

Because here's the secret: gratitude and unworthiness cannot coexist. They are opposites, incompatible. The more you practice gratitude, the less room there is for feelings of inadequacy and insufficiency.

4. Alignment: Embracing Your Light

But perhaps the most important tool of all is that of love. Love is the foundation, the bedrock upon which all other practices rest. Because when you truly love yourself, when you accept and embrace all parts of yourself, the worthy and the unworthy, the light and the dark, something miraculous happens.

You become unshakeable. You become immune to the opinions and judgments of others, to the ups and downs of external circumstances. You tap into a source of strength and resilience and peace that can weather any storm.

Loving yourself doesn't mean you think you're perfect. It doesn't mean you don't make mistakes, have flaws, or face challenges. It means you extend to yourself the same grace, understanding, and forgiveness that you would to a dear friend or a beloved child.

It means you learn to be kind to yourself, to speak to yourself with words of encouragement and appreciation rather than criticism and condemnation. It means you prioritize your own needs and desires, setting healthy boundaries and saying no when necessary.

Most of all, it means you trust yourself. You trust your intuition, your wisdom, your ability to handle whatever life brings. You trust that you are enough, just as you are, in this moment. It's the realization that you are already whole, already complete, already worthy of love and belonging and joy simply because you exist.

Alignment is where your worth starts to ripple out and touch others. When you're living your truth, you naturally inspire and uplift those around you. Your light shines in a way that permits others to shine theirs.

This is the ultimate gift of the journey of worthiness: not just the personal transformation, but the collective healing. As each of us reclaims our worth, we contribute to a global shift, a rising tide of consciousness and compassion.

This is a realization that changes everything. It can transform the way you see yourself, the way you move through the world, the way you relate to others. It can infuse your life with a sense of purpose and meaning and magic that you never knew was possible.

But it's not a one-time event. Unworthiness is a habit, a pattern of thought that has likely been with you for a long time. Overcoming it requires consistent, intentional practice. It requires a willingness to be uncomfortable, to face your fears and your doubts and your insecurities head-on.

It requires courage. The courage to be vulnerable, to be seen, to be authentic. The courage to let go of who you think you should be and embrace who you really are. The courage to shine your light, even when the world feels dark.

But I promise you, it's worth it. Every step, every stumble, every moment of discomfort is leading you closer to your truth, to your power, to your radiance.

And as you walk this path, as you do the sacred work of unlocking your worthiness, remember this: you are not alone. There is a whole community of people out there who are on this journey with you, who are cheering you on, who see your light even when you can't see it yourself.

Reach out to them (and me!). Share your story, your struggles, your triumphs. Let them mirror back to you the beauty and brilliance that you are. Let others remind you of your inherent worthiness, again and again and again.

Because that's what we're here for. To love and support and uplift each other. To help each other remember who we really are. To call each other home.

I went from being the most uncertain, shy, unworthy, unconfident version of myself to a confident, happy, joyous, and proud version of myself today. The journey is worth it. Every single part of it. This is why you're here. You're ready to unlock the real you.

As you integrate the 4 A's into your life, trust that you're exactly where you need to be. Trust that each challenge, each setback, each moment of doubt is an invitation to go deeper, to peel back another layer, to get closer to your core.

And above all, trust in your own light. Trust in the unshakeable, unquenchable, eternal radiance that resides within you. Let it guide you, let it sustain you, let it illuminate your path.

Because your worthiness is not something to be earned or achieved; it's something to be remembered, reclaimed, and embodied. It's your birthright, your true nature, your deepest essence. You are worthy, simply because you are. And that, my friend, is the most liberating truth of all.

Key Takeaways:

- Unworthiness is not a flaw but a messenger pointing you toward your authentic self
- Your worth is inherent—it cannot be earned or lost based on external circumstances
- Practices like self-compassion, gratitude, and boundary-setting actively build self-worth
- Everyone struggles with unworthiness—even those who appear most confident
- The journey to worthiness is both deeply personal and universally connecting

Expert Insights on Worthiness

"Owning our story and loving ourselves through that process is the bravest thing we'll ever do." — Brené Brown, research professor at the University of Houston, who has spent two decades studying courage, vulnerability, shame, and empathy. Her research reveals that people who have a strong sense of worthiness share one thing in common: they believe they are worthy of love and belonging.[2]

"You yourself, as much as anybody in the entire universe, deserve your love and affection." — Buddha. This ancient wisdom aligns with modern positive psychology research showing self-compassion is more strongly associated with positive mental health outcomes than self-esteem.[3]

"The most terrifying thing is to accept oneself completely." — Carl Jung, whose research on the shadow self demonstrates that integrating the parts of ourselves we've rejected is essential for wholeness.[4]

Your Turn: Reflective Free Writing

Take a few minutes now to explore your own relationship with worthiness. Find a quiet space, set a timer for 10 minutes, and write continuously without editing or judging what comes up. You might consider these prompts:

Free Writing Prompts:

- When did I first start feeling unworthy? What messages contributed to that feeling?
- If my inner critic had a voice, what would it say? What would my compassionate self say in response?
- What parts of myself have I been hiding or denying out of fear they make me unworthy?
- Who makes me feel most worthy and accepted? What qualities do they bring to our relationship?

Unlocking Joy

"Don't ask what the world needs. Ask what makes you come alive, and go do it. Because what the world needs is people who have come alive."

– Howard Thurman

Howard Thurman's words echo the essence of unlocking joy in our lives, particularly in our work. But for many of us, including myself, this concept was foreign growing up.

Like many raised by the Generation that weathered the Great Depression and their Baby Boomer children, I inherited the belief that work was about survival—not fulfillment or joy. This generation lived through profound economic hardship and uncertainty, naturally developing a perspective where security trumped satisfaction. Work wasn't meant to be enjoyed; it was a duty, a responsibility, a means to provide.

The values of discipline, responsibility, and perseverance were instilled in me at an early age and created a foundation I'm deeply grateful for—even as I've evolved beyond some of those earlier perspectives.

Growing up in the environment I did, I absorbed the message that achievement required sacrifice. It was what I observed and what I believed for a very long time. I believed that if I did well at school, I was okay inside. If I was leading my company in terms of revenue, I was still okay. External circumstances to dictate an inner state? *What?* But, that's what I believed. So, I studied endlessly and got a 4.0. Luckily I did break out of my shell, albeit slightly, my junior year at the University of Wisconsin-Madison and ended up with a 3.8 GPA. Ha! *Real nice Laura, real nice.* Looking back, I wish I hadn't cared as much about my grades. I wish I had played more, spent more time with friends, and as silly as it sounds, gotten into more trouble.

> **Reflection Moment:** Think about the beliefs about work and success you inherited from previous generations in your family. Which ones have served you well? Which ones might be limiting your capacity for joy?

As I grew older, I started to question many of my beliefs. Was hard work really the only way to achieve success? Was it really necessary to suffer in order to achieve my goals? More importantly, I began to realize that the relentless pursuit of achievement and the pressure to be an overachiever were actually holding me back from finding joy and contentment.

We often chase after what we've been conditioned to view as "success": long hours, exhaustive efforts, relentless striving.

But as a result, we get buried under this identity of being a workaholic, a perfectionist, or an overachiever. Worse yet, we never know our identity because it's been covered by what we *think* we should do and who we should be. The truth is being an overachiever can be a double-edged sword. While it may lead to external markers of success, it can also leave us feeling burnt out, unfulfilled, and disconnected.

Unlike the assembly line jobs of the past, technology has now enabled us to make a living by pursuing our dreams and passions in new ways. Rather than taking on an exhausting job to survive, it's now possible and acceptable to find work today that you truly enjoy. I am finding more and more of my friends are choosing this path and it's exciting to see. My husband's music school business is proof that it is possible to do what you love *and* get paid good money. He's created 18 jobs for music teachers to do what they love. The perception of work is changing (thank you, new generations coming into the workforce!), and with this comes greater freedom and opportunity.

The Neurochemistry of Joy

Neuroscience research has shown us something remarkable about joy: it's not just an emotional state—it physically changes our brains and bodies. When we experience joy, our brains release a cocktail of neurotransmitters including dopamine, serotonin, and endorphins that not only make us feel good but enhance cognitive function, creativity, and problem-solving abilities.[1]

This is where the connection to neurofeedback becomes fascinating. Studies show that people can actually learn to regulate their brain states toward patterns associated with joy and fulfillment.[2] The same neural pathways that light up during neurofeedback training—those associated with presence, flow, and positive emotion—are the ones that activate when we're deeply engaged in meaningful work that brings us joy.

Dr. Richard Davidson, founder of the Center for Healthy Minds, has conducted groundbreaking research showing that positive emotional states like joy are associated with increased activity in the left prefrontal cortex of the brain.[3] The remarkable finding? This pattern of brain activity can be strengthened through practice, just like a muscle.

What this means is simple yet profound: **joy is a skill you can develop.** By consciously choosing activities, thoughts, and experiences that bring you joy, you're literally rewiring your brain to make joy your default state rather than something that happens to you occasionally.

As an executive recruiter in my 30s, I noticed a palpable energy divide between more traditional employees going through the motions and others who seem to draw meaning from their work. The latter exudes enthusiasm, passion, and purpose. They are not doing different jobs, they're approaching their work in a different way. They operate from a place of freedom and alignment with their intuitive wisdom, approaching work not as a list of duties, but as a joyful act of service. They aren't slaves to the clock but are fully present with those they help. They've let go of the need to overachieve and instead focus on being, letting the ever-flowing beauty of the present moment guide them. It's true: it's not what you do, it's HOW you do it.

This brings us back to our core distinction between being and doing. When we're caught in overachievement, we're trapped in constant doing—striving, pushing, proving. Joy, however, emerges from being—from presence, authenticity, and alignment with our true nature.

Can we find more joy in this life if we focus on the how? The answer is a resounding yes. By allowing our unique gifts to shine through this act of service we allow joy to flow through us into all the people around us.

We allow the beingness of us to overshadow the doing.

I speak from experience since I am a recovering overachiever and have gotten wrapped up in the chase of "doing" more than "being" for far longer than I care to admit. My hours were spent cramming as much as I could into each waking hour to please others and meet arbitrary success benchmarks, usually the ones I had placed on myself. But in the process, I realized that I had been missing out on the joy and fulfillment that comes from being in the present moment.

FEATURED PRACTICE: The Joy Reset

Several times throughout your day, practice this simple 30-second joy reset:

1. Pause whatever you're doing
2. Notice your surroundings with all your senses

3. Ask yourself: "What brings me joy in this exact moment?"

4. Breathe deeply as you acknowledge what you discover

Research in positive psychology shows that this type of mindful "joy spotting" practice activates the parasympathetic nervous system, reducing stress hormones and increasing feelings of well-being.[4] By training your brain to regularly seek out moments of joy, you begin to rewire your neural pathways toward positivity and presence.

Stop for a moment, notice your surroundings, and ask yourself what brings you joy in the exact moment. Did you answer the question? Great. I bet it was something simple. I find that by focusing less on striving and more on making meaningful connections with the moment, I am rewiring my brain naturally. I dare you to try this. Start with a couple of times a day and work your way up to a number that feels comfortable to you. Set a reminder on your phone. Over time you'll find that staying in the present moment becomes your natural state. Because it is.

Redefining Success Through Joy

I can't help but wonder how many of us are missing out on finding joy in our days since most of our days are spent in endless meetings and busywork. How many of us are so focused on achieving goals that, if we're honest about them, we don't really care that much about? There is a much bigger issue at hand about the future of work, which many of us are beginning to wake up to. Why choose to spend your precious energy on something that doesn't have a true purpose or fulfillment? What I'm getting at is that I see a revolution taking place from people being at the mercy of their companies, doing everything asked of them, to many taking agency over their careers. Many are instead choosing to become consultants, freelancers, fractional workers, or start their own businesses instead.

So pause for a moment, and ask yourself: Do you feel joy in your work?

Not just joy on certain days or in certain moments, but joy that envelops you like a big hug or feels like you're going to burst from the inside out when you get to do what you do well while at work? If you are rolling your eyes at that, good. Know that that level of joy exists. Be curious about it rather than believing it's not possible.

You can be busy doing and still feel completely disconnected from yourself. But then there are moments when what you're doing aligns effortlessly with who you are. How can you tell? There's no struggle, just flow. Joy replaces effort. That's when you're in your zone of genius.

If you find yourself analyzing what joy means to you in relation to everyday life, let me give you my definition, which you can borrow or alter as you need. True joy is being in the moment. True joy is a deeply rooted state of contentment and fulfillment that comes from aligning with one's authentic self and purpose. It isn't fleeting or dependent on external circumstances; instead, it's an enduring quality that permeates all aspects of what you're doing, no matter the challenges or triumphs you face. And it often requires letting go of the constant pressure to do more.

Let me put it this way: when you're joyful, you're not wishing for the time to pass so you can move onto the next thing. You won't be constantly looking ahead to the next achievement or milestone. Instead, you'll be fully present and engaged in the moment, finding joy in the process, not just the outcome.

From Theory to Transformation: Real Stories of Change

Sarah was a C-suite executive at a Fortune 500 company when we began working together. She had "made it" by all external standards—prestigious position, excellent compensation, impressive title—but felt chronically depleted and disconnected from her life.

"I feel like I'm living someone else's definition of success," she confided during one of our sessions. "I'm exhausted all the time, I barely see my kids, and I can't remember the last time I felt genuinely excited about my work."

Through our coaching, Sarah began implementing small joy practices throughout her day. She started taking actual lunch breaks. She blocked time for deep work rather than bouncing between meetings all day.

She practiced saying "no" to projects that didn't align with her strengths and values.

Eventually, Sarah made the courageous decision to launch her own consulting practice. Today, she structures her days completely differently. She takes a few precious minutes to savor her coffee after getting her kids on the school bus—something that sounds simple but brings her immense joy. She's created an exercise routine that energizes her and leads into deep focus time for client work. The result? She's actually getting more done in fewer hours than she ever did in her executive role, while experiencing substantially more joy.

"The biggest revelation," Sarah told me recently, "is that I don't have to choose between success and joy. When I prioritize joy, I'm actually more effective, more creative, and more impactful in my work."

Your work can be a joyful self-expression. It doesn't have to be a constant grind or a never-ending pursuit of achievement. That doesn't mean that old habits don't creep up on us. They do and that's when we must remember we're evolving beings and that we're prone to wobble. Wobbling is part of the process, so please don't judge yourself when you fall back into old habits or old thought patterns.

Joy as a Choice

Ever since I heard my mentor Brendon Burchard talk about "bringing the joy" as something you SUMMON, my life has never been the same. Brendon, who I later got the honor of being trained by to become a Certified High-Performance Coach, emphasizes that joy isn't something that happens to us—it's something we actively choose to create.

"Joy isn't just an emotion that randomly visits us when circumstances are perfect," Brendon teaches. "It's a choice we make, a muscle we strengthen, and an energy we bring to every situation."[5]

This perspective revolutionized how I approach each day. Rather than waiting for joy to find me when conditions are right, I now understand that I can summon joy regardless of external circumstances. This doesn't mean denying difficult emotions or challenges—it means consciously choosing to bring a quality of lightness, presence, and appreciation to whatever I'm experiencing.

"Bring the joy" is not just a suggestion—it's a practice, a mantra, and ultimately a way of being in the world. It's about deciding in advance that you will be the one who lifts the energy in a room, who finds delight in small moments, who approaches challenges with curiosity rather than dread.

Despite my "hard work is the only work" belief I carried for quite some time, I always felt a pull towards something more joyful. I yearned for work that would allow me to express myself and leave a mark on the world. From a financial standpoint, I didn't see how that was possible for most of my adult working years until I experienced a profound shift in Fall of 2024. I finally believed God would reveal the next steps in a joyful new career–a career that I didn't know was fully possible until I surrendered. A career that is unfolding as I write these very words to you now.

You see, despite being an excellent executive recruiter, something in me had felt off for quite some time. I had been restless for years, lying to myself that I was happy. I had an inner knowing that my greatest gifts were not being used in the greatest magnitude (more on gifts in chapter 4)

I firmly believe that in the next decade, passion, joy, and energy will matter more than any other credentials when choosing what work to do. Rather than a laundry list of skills, companies will hire someone based on their level of joy they have for the work they get to do. Because it's truly a *get to* rather than a have to. Do you see it too? Can you see it shifting before your eyes? Your joy matters just as much as any other skill.

It's about time we redefine work. Work is fulfillment. Work is joyful. Success in work is being you and using your greatest gifts. Success is a lifestyle of your choosing rather than earning a certain title, a certain amount of money or other external indicators. Think about that: how many of us could adjust our lifestyles and have *completely* different lives and careers?

To be clear, I'm not saying you have to leave your full-time job. I am a big fan of side hustles, volunteering, and having other outlets to allow for your creativity and wholeness. But if you've realized that there is more for you, I urge you to begin the exploration.

Case in point, I created a workshop in 2023 called "Pursue Your Purpose" to get people back in alignment with their authentic selves. It was a revamped version of the online course I created back in 2020 called "Your Career, Your Life, On Purpose." I actually lost money in building the course. I wasn't confident in enrolling people. I constantly second-guessed if the product was any good. It took me over four years to adopt a mindset that what I created is worth the price I charge for it. You don't get there overnight. It takes putting the reps to build the skills.

I say that, but I also know there's another way. Maybe it didn't have to take *four* years to learn how to trust myself and charge my worth. Maybe it could have taken a year or six months or less. But that wasn't the path I chose. My free will led me down a winding road that had a number of detours. I could have gotten there sooner. And hint hint to you reader, you can choose to get there sooner. You can get there any way you choose—it can take you a decade, or it can take you a week—the choice is yours.

The 4 A's Framework for Joyful Work

So, how do we navigate this journey toward more fulfilling work? Let's apply our 4 A's Framework to unlocking joy:

1. Awareness: Discovering Your Joy Triggers

Start with self-reflection. Ask yourself, "What makes me forget time?" Begin to notice these moments and activities when you are in a state of flow or feeling energized. This awareness is the first step in noticing what comes easily to you. If it comes easy to you and you enjoy it, you have probably found your joy.

Research in positive psychology by Dr. Mihaly Csikszentmihalyi shows that people who regularly experience "flow"—that state where you're so absorbed in an activity that time seems to disappear—report higher levels of overall life satisfaction.[6] The key is identifying which activities trigger this state for you personally.

Try This:

- Keep a "joy journal" for one week, noting moments when you feel most energized, engaged, and alive
- Ask trusted friends what they observe lights you up
- Notice when you lose track of time—what are you doing in those moments?

2. Attitude: Choosing Joy as Your Default

Then, shift your mindset from "I must work hard to succeed" to "I must work joyfully to succeed." Even if you help one person today, is it worth it? Embrace a positive attitude where you seek joy and growth in your work, not just accomplishments and accolades.

This attitude shift is perhaps the most crucial aspect of unlocking joy. As neuropsychologist Dr. Rick Hanson explains, "The brain is like Velcro for negative experiences but Teflon for positive ones."[7] This negativity bias means we must consciously cultivate an attitude oriented toward joy through regular practice.

FEATURED PRACTICE: The Joy Dance

One of my absolute favorite joy practices takes just two minutes:

1. Choose a song that never fails to lift your spirits
2. Play it at a volume that energizes you
3. Dance with complete abandon for the duration of the song
4. Notice how your mood and energy shift

Research shows that dancing triggers the release of endorphins while reducing levels of cortisol (the stress hormone). According to neuroscientist Dr. Julia Christensen, dance combines the joy-inducing effects of music with the benefits of physical movement, creating a powerful neurochemical shift in your brain.[8] Many of my clients report that this simple two-minute practice completely transforms their emotional state and productivity for hours afterward.

3. Action: Creating Pathways to Joy

Ask yourself, what is one thing I can do today to get closer to joy? What do you love? What are you naturally good at? What activities energize you? How can you do more of what makes you come alive? Realign your current job responsibilities to include more of these elements identified above. Speak to your boss about tailoring your role or taking on a new project—make it a win/

win. Consider starting a side hustle or something that you can do in your free time that allows your soul to sing. No pressure to make money—do it because you love it.

If a job change is needed, start talking to people that already know, like, and trust you. Share with them what you're discovering about yourself and begin exploring roles that align more closely with your passions. Run in the opposite direction if something doesn't light you up. It's not worth it and you'll end up right back where you started. Practice letting go of the overachiever mentality. Remind yourself that it's okay to focus on doing work that feels meaningful and fulfilling, even if it doesn't always lead to external markers of success. Trust yourself, trust yourself, trust yourself.

Try This:

- Identify one task in your current job that brings you joy, and find ways to expand it
- Have a conversation with your manager about how your role could evolve to better align with your strengths
- Start a small side project purely for the joy of it, with no pressure for it to "succeed"

4. Alignment: Designing a Joy-Centered Life

Finally, create a joy-focused routine. Integrate small practices into your daily routine that bring you joy. It could be a morning ritual, a short mid-day activity that energizes you, or an evening reflection on what brought you joy that day. Make joy a priority, not just an afterthought. For me this looks like a 30-minute walk to raise my vibration first thing in the morning, reading for 20 minutes in the sauna before I pick my youngest son from daycare, or turning on one of my favorite songs in the car and belting it! And let's not forget one of my favorites: hugging a tree. Yes, I'm that person. Weird is cool. At least that's what I tell my four sons with the hopes that they embrace their inner weirdness.

Your joy practices will be different than mine, and that's a good thing. Based on your passions and interests, choose joy practices that feel right for you. They don't have to take up much time either. The key is consistency—small moments of intentional joy regularly practiced are far more effective than occasional grand gestures.

Try This:

- Design a morning ritual that sets a joyful tone for your day
- Create boundaries around technologies or activities that drain your joy
- Schedule "joy appointments" with yourself throughout your week—small pockets of time dedicated to what energizes you

Understand that by finding joy, you're not only enhancing your own life but also positively impacting those around you. Joy is contagious; it fosters creativity, collaboration, and overall well-being. When you let go of the "shoulds" and instead focus on doing work that feels meaningful and fulfilling, you inspire others to do the same.

The world doesn't just need more "workers." It needs more people who have come alive in their work. Your light, in alignment with your truest self, can ignite incredible change. It's a journey towards work that doesn't just pay the bills but enriches your soul and, in turn, enriches the world. It's not just a career path; it's your life's path. And trust me, it's worth walking.

Key Takeaways:

- Joy is not an accident—it's a choice we can make regardless of circumstances
- Your brain can be physically rewired for joy through consistent practice
- Small, intentional joy practices throughout the day can transform your experience of work and life
- Being versus doing: Joy emerges from presence and alignment, not from constant achievement
- You can influence your workplace toward joy or create new work arrangements that better support your wellbeing
- Joy is contagious—when you prioritize joy, you give others permission to do the same

Expert Insights on Joy in Work

"The only way to do great work is to love what you do. If you haven't found it yet, keep looking. Don't settle." — Steve Jobs, who revolutionized multiple industries by following his curiosity and passion.[9]

"Joy does not simply happen to us. We have to choose joy and keep choosing it every day." — Henri Nouwen, whose research and writings on spirituality emphasize joy as an intentional practice rather than a random occurrence.[10]

"Pleasure is always derived from something outside you, whereas joy arises from within." — Eckhart Tolle, whose work on presence and consciousness has transformed our understanding of authentic happiness.[11]

"When you're interested in something, you pay attention to it. When you're passionate about something, it pays attention to you." — Brendon Burchard, high performance coach and researcher on human motivation and fulfillment.[12]

Your Turn: Reflective Free Writing

Take a few minutes now to explore your own relationship with joy. Find a quiet space and write continuously without editing or judging what comes up. You might consider these prompts:

Free Writing Prompts:

- When was the last time I felt completely joyful? What was I doing, and with whom?
- If I designed a workday filled with maximum joy, what would it include? What would it exclude?
- What small joy practices could I realistically integrate into my daily routine starting tomorrow?
- How might prioritizing joy change the way I feel?

Unlocking Your Gifts

"The meaning of life is to find your gift. The purpose of life is to give it away."

– Pablo Picasso

In the whirlwind of life, where the relentless pursuit of "more" often clouds our judgment, our authentic gifts—those unique talents and abilities that are purely us—can get lost in the noise. We struggle to keep up with the pace of our fast-paced world, merged with our desire to be accepted. The essence of who we are frequently gets shunted to the backburner, hidden under obligations, stifled by fear, or perhaps even hoarded away like a guarded treasure. But what if you were to honor your gifts, allowing them to shine in all their glory? What if you were to let go of the tendency to underestimate yourself and your abilities?

Marianne Williamson's iconic poem "Our Deepest Fear" beautifully encapsulates this idea. Please google it and read it now. It's beautiful. Marianne Williamson suggests that our greatest fear isn't that we're inadequate, but that we're actually more powerful than we can imagine. We often ask ourselves, "Who am I to be brilliant, talented, or extraordinary?" But she flips this question on its head, asking instead, "Who are you not to be?" She reminds us that we all possess an inner light, a spark of the divine, and that we have a responsibility to let it shine.

Too often, we underestimate ourselves, doubting our potential and the value of our unique gifts. We compare, diminish, and convince ourselves we don't measure up. But when we do this, we not only limit our own growth—we deprive the world of the contributions only we can make.

> **Reflection Moment:** Think about a time when you downplayed your abilities or dismissed a compliment about your talents. What were you feeling in that moment? What might have changed if you had fully embraced that recognition?

I know this trap well. For the first ten years of my career, I tried to emulate the executives around me—older, business-savvy men who thrived on strategy and data. Meanwhile, my success in recruiting stemmed from something entirely different: understanding people through my intuition. I had a knack for getting candidates to open up to me quickly, diving into the psychology behind their motivations. It felt effortless—fun, even. I could interview 20 people and intuitively know who would get hired.

But I kept that to myself. Instead of embracing my gift, I feared it wasn't "business-focused" enough. Intuition felt too soft, too "hippy-dippy" for the corporate world.

At least, that was the story I told myself for far too long.

I constantly beat myself up, convinced I wasn't as polished or strategic as other "successful" executive recruiters. I spent years pretending to be like them—until I met someone who changed everything.

She was different. She led our office in revenue, yet spent more time talking about life than business with her candidates and clients. I was beyond fascinated. I studied her every move, and eventually, I worked up the courage to ask her for coffee. She became my mentor, and she shared a truth that reshaped my entire outlook:

"Stop trying to be anyone but yourself. When you fully embrace who you are, you'll naturally attract the right people. It's almost like magic."

And she was right. Slowly, I let go of the shame around my gift of intuition.

Discovering Your Gifts: A Starting Point

How do we discover our gifts? If the word gift doesn't resonate, try strength or talent. But I love *gift* because it implies something given from above—something entrusted to us by God.

Understanding your gifts is key to personal and career growth. When you recognize what comes naturally to you, you can align your life and work in a way that brings joy instead of resistance.

FEATURED PRACTICE: The Gift Mirror

Here's a simple way to start discovering your gifts through the eyes of others:

1. **Reach out:** Text or email a few trusted friends, colleagues, or family members with this question: "What do you see as my greatest gift?"
2. **Receive openly:** When responses come in, resist the urge to dismiss or downplay them.
3. **Notice your feelings:** Pay attention to your emotional reaction to each response. Which gifts feel most aligned with your sense of self? Which ones surprise you?
4. **Look for patterns:** As you gather responses, notice recurring themes. These patterns often point to your most visible and impactful gifts.

Psychologist Dr. Robert Biswas-Diener's research on strengths recognition shows that we often overlook our most natural talents because they come so easily to us that we assume everyone possesses them.[1] Having others reflect our gifts back to us can reveal blind spots in our self-awareness and help us embrace abilities we've been taking for granted.

This exercise can be a powerful way to move past the underestimator mindset and start recognizing the true value of your gifts. So go ahead and text five more people. And enjoy those responses you get.

Gifts in Action

About a year ago I got introduced to a woman who had been looking for work for 15+ months. She had previously hired other career coaches and LinkedIn experts to help her position herself for a new job. But everyone she met with told her to do things that didn't feel in alignment with who she was. They said she should position herself for business analyst roles. Thus, she changed her resume and LinkedIn to reflect that. Six months later, no job bites.

When I met with her, I could see clearly she's a generalist and her gift is taking complex issues and breaking them into bite-size pieces for teams to rally behind and turn into processes that the team can follow. I delivered her a new LinkedIn narrative pro bono and when I presented it, she began to cry. They were happy tears, of course. *"Thank you, Laura. No one has ever seen me the way you see me. You captured words that make my gifts come alive,"* she said.

I have no doubt that our hour spent together where I showed her exactly how her gifts came alive in her past work experiences was the fuel that she needed. Many of us tend to doubt ourselves. We have been conditioned to believe we have to act the part in order to receive admiration or accolades. Sometimes all we need is for someone to act as a mirror for us to see our gifts in a new light. Embracing what comes naturally to you is a gift in and of itself. The next step is allowing ourselves to accept those gifts as truth. This woman found a new job one month later. *Gift activated.*

Honoring Your Gifts in Every Season

Activating our gifts might mean saying no to what the world (society) says is "success" to choose what success means to you. Early in my career, I thought I wanted a manager role since it was the next common-sense step. But as I began interviewing potential hires for my team, I had a revelation. The time I'd need to train up and develop a new hire would detract from what I really wanted most: more time with my family. If I was being honest with myself, I knew I had so much to give to younger professionals and could have built an amazing team, but I didn't want that at that time in my life. I was building a family and only had so much energy to give. I chose to give my extra energy to my kids, knowing there will be a time in the future I'll be able to pour into a team.

I had to grapple with my ego, acknowledging that I was intentionally opting out of a big promotion, a decision that would likely bruise my ego at future company gatherings because those were the employees that were most celebrated. But inside I know I made the right call, and I honor my younger self for being strong enough to not give in to the societal pressure to be "more worthy" if I had a large team and bigger title.

I made a choice aligned with my values and season of life. And in doing so, I let go of the tendency to underestimate my own gifts and passions. I'm an incredible networker and relationship builder. I love working directly with my clients. If I were building a team, that would mean more time teaching and coaching vs. direct client interaction. I had to trust that following my intuition and honoring my unique strength as an individual performer was more important than conforming to societal expectations.

We often seek external validation of our worthiness from titles, money, or others' opinions. But worth comes from within. Is taking the next job up the hierarchy really what you want? Or is it something else? Societal expectations often conflict with individual authenticity. Acting a part may offer momentary satisfaction but can ultimately lead to misalignment.

I can't tell you how many times I've had this conversation with women who are in their childrearing years. They call me and are exhausted because they took a bigger job but in doing that, they have less time with their children and spouse. I have literally told hundreds of women that it's okay to take an "easier" job for a season. You don't have to win all the awards at work right now. You might choose a whole different category: being the best mom and best spouse you can be. Honor yourself. Honor where you're being called.

The same goes for adults taking care of their aging parents. It's ok to not do it all. You might not want that promotion or more responsibility if you have other pressing priorities that, let's be honest, are more important. And that's okay to ask for less in other areas of your life. It doesn't mean you're underestimating yourself or your potential. It means you're honoring your priorities and values.

Reflection Moment: In what areas of your life have you been pursuing society's definition of success rather than your own? What would change if you redefined success based on your values, season of life, and natural gifts?

Reconnecting with Forgotten Gifts

I discovered writing in my journal was a core gift of mine in my young adulthood, but then I forgot about it for close to 20 years. The bookstore's self-help section spoke to me as a young girl and I filled diaries with inspiring quotes and dreams for the future. Today I can look back and see that it was all designed to point me in the direction of writing, sharing, and inspiring others. I love it and do it so naturally. But I denied it for so long. My countless hours of journaling and reading inspirational texts in my young adulthood had a purpose. And the things you do in your spare time (whether now or decades ago) have a purpose as well. Don't underestimate the value and potential of those natural inclinations. Rekindle something you used to do and see what happens.

Try This:

- Think about activities you loved as a child or young adult but abandoned as you got older
- Choose one of these activities and commit to exploring it again for just 15 minutes this week
- Notice how you feel during and after engaging with this forgotten passion

See your gifts as a blessing, not something you created alone. A couple of years ago I started listening to the John Maxwell leadership podcast. Something I learned about John is that after every speech he takes a moment to thank God for allowing his teaching gift to flow through him. He knows it's not about him but rather what flows through him. He can't take credit for it. When I first heard this, I found it so humbling. And the more I thought about it, the more I started to believe that we're all channels for the divine to pass through us.

Your gifts are blessings. So please honor them and share them generously.

Connecting with your unique gifts and using them more often is one way to reclaim our inner light to shine brighter in this world. Your talents are not yours alone; they're meant to uplift others. As you learn to appreciate your abilities and share them generously, you'll be amazed by how much value you contribute. Your distinctiveness is a precious gift only you can offer the world. And it's time to stop underestimating that gift.

The Science of Recognizing Your Gifts

Research in positive psychology reveals something fascinating about our natural talents and strengths. According to Dr. Martin Seligman, founder of positive psychology, people who use their "signature strengths"—their natural gifts—in daily life report higher levels of happiness, engagement, and meaning.[2] These signature strengths are not just things we're good at; they're activities and abilities that energize us and feel authentic to our core identity.

What's particularly interesting is how often we overlook our most significant gifts. Researchers at the VIA Institute on Character found that people frequently undervalue their top strengths precisely because these abilities come so naturally that they assume everyone possesses them.[3] This "gift blindness" can prevent us from fully developing and sharing our most valuable contributions.

Neurologically, when we engage in activities aligned with our natural gifts, our brains show increased flow states—characterized by complete absorption, timelessness, and reduced self-consciousness. During these states, the brain's default mode network (responsible for self-criticism and rumination) becomes less active, while creative and performance networks become more synchronized.[4]

The 4 A's Framework for Unlocking Your Gifts

We're on the verge of so many more people fully stepping into their light. But we can't light up the world if our flame is depleted. To help you unlock your gifts and let them shine, let's break it down using the 4 A's Framework:

1. Awareness: Recognize Your Unique Talents

It's crucial to recognize and appreciate that what comes naturally to you doesn't come naturally to others. For many, self-awareness is the first hurdle to overcome, especially if you've been in the habit of doubting yourself. Reach out to a circle of 5-10 friends, past colleagues, or family who know you well enough. Ask them, "What is my number one gift?" as discussed earlier in the chapter.

Gather these reflections, set some quiet time aside, and really digest the feedback you receive. This exercise doesn't just make you aware of your own gifts; it shows you how others value your uniqueness, often in ways you've never considered.

According to research by the Gallup Organization, people who focus on developing their natural talents rather than fixing their weaknesses are six times more likely to be engaged in their work and three times more likely to report having an excellent quality of life.[5] Awareness of your gifts is the foundation for this engagement and well-being.

Try This:

- Keep a "gift journal" for one week, noting activities that give you energy rather than drain it
- Pay attention to tasks that feel effortless or cause you to lose track of time
- Notice when others repeatedly ask for your help in specific areas—these requests often point to your unique gifts

2. Attitude: Embrace Your Gifts Without Apology

Once you're aware of your unique gifts, the next step is developing the right attitude towards them. Owning your gifts doesn't equate to arrogance; it's about honoring your unique capabilities. Think of your talents as tools in a toolbox. They're not bragging rights but rather instruments that can be used to build something greater—not just for you but also for those around you. Keep a 'gifts journal' where you note down daily instances where your gifts have come into play. This kind of recognition nurtures a quiet confidence that inspires you to share your gifts with the world.

FEATURED PRACTICE: The Gifts Without Apology Exercise

1. **Write a declaration:** Create a simple statement acknowledging your gifts without diminishing them. For example: "I have a natural gift for [your gift], and I choose to honor and develop it."
2. **Practice saying it aloud:** Stand in front of a mirror and say your declaration confidently, without adding qualifiers like "but," "just," or "kind of."
3. **Notice resistance:** Pay attention to any discomfort, embarrassment, or urge to downplay your gift as you make this declaration.
4. **Repeat daily:** Practice this declaration every morning for one week, allowing yourself to become more comfortable with owning your gifts.

Research by Dr. Amy Cuddy of Harvard University demonstrates that the way we speak about ourselves not only influences how others perceive us but actually changes our own self-perception and even our physiology.[6] By deliberately practicing confident acknowledgment of our gifts, we can overcome the socialized tendency to underestimate our abilities.

3. Action: Put Your Gifts to Work

Understanding and respecting your gifts is great, but these insights are of little value unless translated into action. Whether you incorporate your talents into your professional life, channel them into your hobbies, or use them in volunteer opportunities, the key is to make them an integral part of your daily existence. Invest in courses, workshops, or any other resources that can hone your gifts further. Take that step out of your comfort zone, and embrace the exhilarating uncertainty that comes with growth.

Psychologist Mihaly Csikszentmihalyi's research on "flow" states—those moments when we're completely absorbed in an activity that perfectly matches our skills—shows that regularly engaging in activities aligned with our natural gifts is essential for psychological well-being and happiness.[7]

Try This:

- Identify one way you could use your gifts more fully in your day
- Create a small project outside work that leverages your unique talents
- Seek out learning opportunities that would enhance your natural gifts rather than fixing weaknesses

4. Alignment: Let Your Gifts Guide Your Choices

Being in alignment means your internal and external worlds are in harmony. It's about living authentically, honoring your true self in the choices you make, the work you do, the language you use, and the way you interact with the world. Finding this alignment might entail making some tough decisions: perhaps turning down a high-paying job that conflicts with your values, or choosing a path less traveled that resonates more closely with your true self. But the rewards—inner peace, satisfaction, and a sense of purpose—far outweigh the sacrifices.

Research in career development shows that people who align their work with their natural talents and values report significantly higher job satisfaction and show greater resilience in the face of workplace challenges.[8] This alignment creates a virtuous cycle where using your gifts generates positive outcomes, which in turn reinforces your confidence in those gifts.

Try This:

- Review your major life decisions of the past year—how many honored your natural gifts?
- Consider upcoming choices through the lens of your gifts— which options would allow them to flourish?
- Create boundaries around activities or commitments that consistently pull you away from using your gifts

The Ripple Effect of Honoring Your Gifts

Uncovering, owning, and utilizing your true gifts is not just a self-serving endeavor. It is a radical act of contribution to a world desperate for the uniqueness only you can offer. One's talents can become their lifeline out of darkness. Declare and own your gifts, it is your birthright. And let go of the tendency to underestimate their value and potential. You are capable of so much more than you often give yourself credit for. It's time to step into your power and let your light shine.

When you honor your gifts, you create ripple effects that extend far beyond yourself. By giving yourself permission to shine, you implicitly give others permission to do the same. Your courage in embracing your gifts can inspire countless others to recognize and share their own unique talents.

Key Takeaways:

- Your unique gifts are what the world needs most from you—and they're often what comes most naturally
- The tendency to underestimate our gifts often stems from their effortlessness in our own experience
- Success should be defined on your terms, considering your values, season of life, and natural gifts
- Your gifts may evolve or express differently in various life seasons—this evolution is natural and valuable
- Honoring your gifts is not selfish—it's a necessary contribution to a world that needs your unique light

Expert Insights on Gifts and Talents

"Everybody is a genius. But if you judge a fish by its ability to climb a tree, it will live its whole life believing that it is stupid." — Albert Einstein, whose work on relativity revolutionized physics and who recognized the importance of honoring diverse forms of intelligence and talent.[9]

"Your talent is God's gift to you. What you do with it is your gift back to God." — Leo Buscaglia, whose research and teachings on human connection and love emphasize the spiritual dimension of our natural gifts.[10]

"Hide not your talents, they for use were made. What's a sundial in the shade?" — Benjamin Franklin, whose diverse talents as inventor, scientist, writer, and statesman demonstrate the power of embracing multiple gifts.[11]

"The privilege of a lifetime is being who you are." — Joseph Campbell, whose research on the hero's journey revealed that embracing one's authentic gifts is central to finding meaning and purpose.[12]

Your Turn: Reflective Free Writing

Take a few minutes now to explore your relationship with your unique gifts. Find a quiet space, set a timer for 10 minutes, and write continuously without editing or judging what comes up. You might consider these prompts:

Free Writing Prompts:

- What activities or abilities have always felt natural to me, almost like breathing?
- When do I feel most alive, engaged, and in flow? What gifts am I using in those moments?
- What gifts did I express freely as a child but have set aside as an adult?
- In what ways have I been underestimating my natural talents? What stories have I been telling myself about them?

PART II

The Path to Authentic Impact

Unlocking Confidence

"All our dreams can come true, if we have the courage to pursue them."

– Walt Disney

I n the age of social media highlight reels, comparison is nearly inescapable. We scroll, we like, we compare. It's automatic—seeping beyond our screens into workplace conversations, family gatherings, and casual outings with friends. The pressure is relentless, the cycle incessant. But have you ever stopped to consider the cost?

Comparison may seem harmless, but it's a silent thief. It steals joy, erodes confidence, and limits our potential. It's one of the biggest roadblocks to authenticity and personal fulfillment. The exhausting battle to remind ourselves that our worth isn't measured by how we stack up against others but by how true we are to ourselves—it's real.

Some days, I need deep breaths just to remember this truth. Because let's be honest: Society doesn't make it easy.

I learned this lesson the hard way.

My first job out of college was at Target headquarters. Deep down, I knew it wasn't the right fit. But in October of my senior year, they offered me $48,000—an incredible salary for 2005. Everyone around me reinforced that it was the right, practical decision. So, I ignored my gut.

Have you ever ignored your gut feeling? How did that work out for you?

> **Reflection Moment:** Think about a time when you ignored your intuition to follow a path others approved of. What happened? How did it feel in your body? What did you learn from that experience?

You can probably guess how my Target story ends. By not listening to myself, I had to learn the lesson the hard way. From day one, I was thrown into new employee training with 40 other business analysts. The environment felt like business school all over again—peers competing against peers. It was a breeding ground for comparison and self-doubt.

I was determined to be the best. I studied late into the night, memorizing manuals to keep up. But it didn't come naturally, and I didn't enjoy it. Three months in, the pressure cracked me open. I had my first panic attack—one of the scariest moments of my life.

My heart raced. My chest tightened. The room spun. I was terrified. I didn't know what to do other than stay in bed. The panic turned into a long, depressive era for me and I had to take a medical leave of absence from Target.

For months, I barely left my apartment or saw people. There were weeks where I could hardly leave my room, let alone the apartment. Medication and therapy eventually helped me function at about 50% of my normal capacity, but it took a long time for my normal disposition to return. It was one of the darkest times of my life—I was a shell of myself with little to no hope for the future.

Looking back, I can see how much of my anxiety and depression stemmed from constantly comparing myself to others and feeling like I didn't measure up. I was trying to force myself into a mold that didn't fit, all because I thought it was what I was supposed to do, what would make me look successful in the eyes of others. But in the process, I lost touch with my own needs, desires, and sense of self.

The Neuroscience of Comparison

Research has shown that frequent comparison with others can lead to feelings of envy, jealousy, and dissatisfaction with our own lives. Over time, this can create a cycle of negativity that impacts our mental health, relationships, and overall well-being. By constantly focusing on what others have, we inadvertently undermine our own worth and blind ourselves to our unique gifts and talents.

From a neurological perspective, social comparison activates the same brain regions associated with physical pain.[1] When we compare ourselves unfavorably to others, our brains register this as a genuine threat to our well-being. This triggers the body's stress response, releasing cortisol and other stress hormones that, over time, can contribute to anxiety, depression, and even physical illness.

What's particularly interesting is that social media intensifies this effect. Studies show that passive scrolling through others' carefully curated highlights activates more comparison-related brain activity than active engagement or real-world interactions.[2] This helps explain why many people report feeling worse about themselves after spending time on social media platforms.

FEATURED PRACTICE:
The Comparison Interrupt

When you catch yourself in a comparison spiral, try this three-step practice to interrupt the pattern:

1. **Notice**: Become aware that you're comparing. Simply name it: "I'm comparing myself again."
2. **Breathe**: Take three slow, deep breaths while placing a hand on your heart.
3. **Redirect**: Ask yourself, "What's one thing I appreciate about my unique journey right now?"

Research by Dr. Kristin Neff shows that this type of self-compassion practice can reduce the negative emotional impact of comparison by activating the parasympathetic nervous system (our "rest and digest" response) and releasing oxytocin, which counteracts stress hormones.[3]

Right now, consider the ways you might be comparing yourself to others. Take a deep breath and ask yourself: Is this comparison helping me grow, or is it holding me back? Write down one thing you appreciate about yourself at this moment. I'll wait. Okay, you got it?

A turning point came when a friend encouraged me to read a book called Do What You Are. This led me to explore human resources, and I stumbled upon a recruiting coordinator ad on Monster.com. I got hired and started to get my mojo back, enjoying talking to people on the phone and eavesdropping on interviews that the recruiters I supported conducted. Nine months later, I was promoted to become a recruiter, a position that paid $10,000 less than my job at Target. But I didn't care at all. I was in learning mode, and it felt right. I was doing a job aligned with my interests and strengths, not to mention it brought way less stress. I was listening to my joy and knew it was closer to my right path. The anxiety was no longer paralyzing my body causing panic attacks or sleepless nights. Slowly but surely I began to feel more like myself.

That rough spot in my early adulthood taught me a valuable lesson: it's up to me to chart my own course, not follow some cookie-cutter version of success defined by others. I had to stop comparing myself to other people and instead focus on what felt right to me. At Target, I hit rock bottom because I was stuck in a comparison and competing mentality—and I didn't even like the job! That was the most maddening part. Why did I let myself care so much about what others thought? Why did I let my parents and other voices tell me this was the right path when deep down inside I knew it wasn't? It took a long bout of anxiety and depression before I realized I needed to take control and find work aligned with who I am and what I enjoy.

The lesson here? The quicker you explore what intrinsically interests you, the sooner you'll find alignment. Sometimes, the path may not be obvious. For instance, a friend of mine started drawing birds just for fun, which eventually led to her creating a children's book and product line fueled entirely by her passion. This transformation happened over several years. So, don't put pressure on yourself to immediately turn your interests into a full-time job. As Joseph Campbell taught us, "follow your bliss," and you never know where it may lead. Most importantly, don't compare your journey to anyone else's. Your path is uniquely yours.

When I moved into a full-desk executive recruiter, the name of the game was all about selling. Selling clients on why they should work with you and selling candidates on why they should consider the job you were working on. Selling people, the most unpredictable product that exists might be the hardest sales job of them all. And at these search firms we're ranked by revenue. Enter, breeding ground for comparison. It is a constant practice to remind myself that I am not my number.

And yet, this has been some of the hardest inner work I've ever had to do. For years, I attached my worth to my ranking, letting company leaderboards dictate how I felt about myself. Past Laura was triggered every time she saw the numbers. Every single time, the same old belief resurfaced: You are only as valuable as your results.

But now I see the deeper truth—the pain, the struggle, the frustration were never punishments. They were invitations. An opportunity to unlearn the conditioning that told me that I had to earn my worthiness.

You are not defined by what you do. You get to define who you are.

Being over doing. Presence over performance. Love over striving.

This is the soul's journey—to transcend the illusions of success, to remember what truly matters. I hear my soul whisper: You already know why you're here. But the ego doesn't go quietly. It screams back: Keep striving. Keep performing. Keep achieving. That's how you prove your worth.

The Shift from Ego to Soul

Old Laura—the Laura of 24 months ago—would have panicked at the thought of falling behind. She needed to be at the top of the rankings. So she worked. And worked. And worked.

At the cost of her inner peace. At the cost of her family. At the cost of her health some days. She was obsessed with proving herself. The thought on repeat: I must get back on top to be okay.

Do you see the pattern?

Do. Do. Do. Work. Work. Work. Force. Force. Force. Control. Control. Control.

For what? At what cost?

But today, I choose differently. I listen to my soul instead of my ego. The ego wants safety, predictability, and control. But I don't want safety anymore. I want to be expansive, wild, and free. I want to look back at my life and know that I became all that I could be. I desire to be the peak version of me that God created me to be.

And so, I surrender. There's a softness now, a peace settling over me. I can see it so clearly—all the personal development work I've done on myself has led me to this exact moment. These circumstances didn't happen to me. I created them, designed them, called them in—for my soul's growth. I truly believe I caused my own suffering so that I could transcend it.

I imagine that fearful version of myself in my mind's eye, the one who was desperate for validation, and I want to hold her in my arm and tell her:

You are enough. Just as you are. You don't need the numbers, the rankings, the accolades to prove your worth. You never did.

Today business flows to me effortlessly. Opportunities appear at the right time. I no longer fight to swim upstream—I let the river carry me downstream.

And for the first time in a long time… I am at peace.

We can't find our version of peace if we're constantly comparing ourselves to others and trying to live up to their standards.

Beyond Surface-Level Comparisons

I often have to pause and question myself: "Why are you making assumptions about people you don't even know, Laura?" Because the truth is, we never really know what's going on behind the scenes in someone else's life. Those people I envy on social media or in my workplace could be struggling with their own demons, their own insecurities, their own battles. Comparison truly is the thief of joy.

I now realize how much of my stress and anxiety stemmed from fear: fear of disappointing my parents, fear of wasting my education, fear of not making enough money for my family. But I have to ask myself, "Do you want to let other people's judgments dictate your life, or do you want to define success on your own terms?"

When the comparison voice arises, sit in awareness. Zoom out for a second and pretend like you're watching yourself in a movie. Become hyper-aware of the comparison. You now have the power to choose something else. Choose to find your breath and come into your heart. Find your center. The real you. Whether through meditation, nature walks, or even in the company of certain individuals, come back to your center. Do whatever it takes to connect with your inner self, the one that can acknowledge that no one else's path is equal to your own.

This is a hard one to conquer, but with awareness and repetition, you can do it.

From Theory to Transformation: Real Stories of Change

The devastating effects of comparison—and the transformative power of letting it go—isn't just part of my story. I see it play out with my clients every day. Tim's journey is a perfect example.

Tim hired me as his coach after leaving a prestigious corporate marketing position to launch his own consulting business as a Fractional CMO (Chief Marketing Officer). On paper, he had everything he needed to succeed: impressive credentials, deep industry knowledge, and a solid network. But after our first few sessions, I could see what was really holding him back—he was trapped in constant comparison to other consultants in his field.

"I look at their websites and LinkedIn profiles," he confessed during one of our early sessions, "and they all seem so polished, so confident. They have these perfect case studies and testimonials. Then I look at what I'm putting together and it feels... inadequate."

This comparison mindset manifested as perfectionism and imposter syndrome. Tim would spend weeks refining his service offerings, tweaking his website, and overthinking every potential client interaction. Despite all his preparation, four months into our work together, he still hadn't secured a single paying client.

During a particularly honest coaching session, I decided to challenge him directly.

"Tim, why don't you have a paying client yet?" I asked.

He launched into explanations about needing to refine his approach and perfect his materials.

"Those are excuses," I told him gently but firmly. "If you wanted to have a client by now, you would have one. But there are some blocks holding you back that are really important for us to address. Your overthinking and need for perfection are going to keep you stuck if we don't tackle them head-on."

I shared a perspective that shifted something in him: "If I were in your shoes, I'd have already gotten at least one client—not just for the income, but to justify investing in coaching for another six months to help break through these limiting beliefs."

He looked at me, speechless.

There was the resistance. Comparison had created such deep insecurity that he couldn't imagine putting himself out there before everything was "perfect."

But something must have clicked overnight.

The next morning, I received a text from him that I'll never forget: "You're right. I've been hiding behind perfectionism because I'm terrified of not measuring up. But I realize now that waiting until I feel 'ready' means I'll be waiting forever. I'm going to reach out to those three prospects today. Thanks for the push I needed."

Over the next six months, Tim secured not one but three new clients. The transformation was remarkable. As he stopped comparing himself to others and started focusing on the unique value he could provide, his authentic strengths began to shine through. His communications became more genuine, his proposals more confident, and his client relationships more meaningful.

"The irony," Tim told me later, "is that by stopping the comparison and just being myself, I actually stand out more. Clients tell me they chose me because I felt real to them—not like I was trying to fit some consultant mold."

Tim's story powerfully illustrates how letting go of comparison isn't just a mental exercise—it unlocks real-world results. By releasing the need to measure up to others in his field, he could finally invite his authentic self to shine through. And that authentic self was exactly what his clients were looking for.

The Psychology of Comparison and Confidence

Research in social psychology provides fascinating insights into how comparison affects our self-perception and confidence. According to Dr. Leon Festinger's Social Comparison Theory, we have an innate drive to evaluate ourselves by comparing our abilities and opinions to others.[4] While this can sometimes motivate improvement, it often leads to what psychologists call "compare and despair" thinking patterns.

What's particularly interesting is that we tend to engage in what researchers call "upward comparisons"—comparing ourselves to those we perceive as doing better than us—rather than "downward comparisons" to those who might be struggling more.[5] This selective comparison creates a skewed perception of where we stand and can significantly undermine our confidence and satisfaction.

However, research also shows that developing a strong internal locus of evaluation—basing our self-worth on our own standards rather than external comparisons—correlates with greater psychological well-being, resilience, and authentic confidence.[6] This is good news because it means that by intentionally shifting our focus from others to ourselves, we can cultivate genuine confidence that isn't dependent on how we stack up against anyone else.

The 4 A's Framework for Breaking Free from Comparison

1. Awareness: Recognize the Comparison Trap

Start by becoming conscious of when you fall into the comparison trap and how it impacts your well-being. Keep a 'Comparison Diary' for a week, noting instances when you felt compelled to measure your life against others. Detail your emotional state and thoughts during these times. This exercise will help you realize how comparison subtly, yet profoundly, affects your overall well-being.

Studies in mindfulness show that simply becoming aware of thought patterns like comparison can create space between the trigger and our response, enabling us to choose a different reaction.[7] This awareness is the essential first step in breaking free from automatic comparison habits.

When working with Tim, our first breakthrough came through awareness exercises. I had him track every time he visited a competitor's website or social media profile, noting his emotional state before and after. This simple practice revealed how these comparison moments were draining his energy and confidence multiple times daily. Awareness of this pattern was essential before he could change it.

Try This:

- Set a "comparison alert" on your phone to check in with yourself three times daily and notice if you're in comparison mode

- After using social media, journal about any comparison thoughts that arose
- Ask a trusted friend to gently point out when you make self-diminishing comparisons in conversation

2. Attitude: Cultivate Self-Compassion

As you become more aware of comparison's negative impact, cultivate a more compassionate attitude towards yourself. Shift from asking, "how do I measure up to them?" to "How can I be kinder to myself?" Create a 'Celebration List' of your accomplishments and growth milestones, no matter how small. Reflect on this list regularly, fostering gratitude for your unique journey and who you're becoming.

Dr. Kristin Neff's research has conclusively shown that self-compassion—treating ourselves with the same kindness we would offer a good friend—is more effective for building genuine confidence than self-esteem approaches based on positive self-evaluation or comparison to others.[8]

FEATURED PRACTICE:
The Self-Compassion Letter

1. **Identify a comparison trigger**: Think of an area where you frequently compare yourself to others and feel inadequate.
2. **Write as a friend**: Write a letter to yourself as if you were writing to a deeply loved friend facing the

same feelings of inadequacy. What would you say to them? How would you remind them of their value?

3. **Use compassionate language**: Include phrases like "It's understandable that you feel this way" and "You're not alone in this struggle."

4. **Highlight unique strengths**: Remind yourself of the unique qualities and strengths you bring that have nothing to do with comparison.

5. **Read it aloud**: When you finish writing, read your letter aloud to yourself, allowing the compassionate words to really sink in.

Research shows that this exercise activates neural pathways associated with self-soothing and security, helping to rewire the brain's habitual comparison patterns.[9]

3. Action: Create Healthy Boundaries

Take concrete steps to reduce exposure to comparison triggers. Consider a social media cleanse or unfollowing accounts that make you feel inferior. Many of my friends who've left social media completely report feeling calmer, less stressed, and more at peace. Beyond digital detox, focus on reconnecting with yourself through mindfulness practices, hobbies, or community service. Choose activities that resonate with your true self and reinforce your sense of self-worth.

Studies have shown that limiting social media use to 30 minutes per day led to significant reductions in loneliness, depression, and comparison-related anxiety.[10] Sometimes the most powerful action we can take is creating boundaries around the inputs that trigger our comparison mindset.

For Tim, action meant creating strict boundaries around his industry research. We developed a "market awareness schedule" where he would only check competitor websites once weekly for 30 minutes. More importantly, he committed to reaching out to one potential client every day—even before he felt "ready." This shifted his focus from comparison to connection, with remarkable results. Within three weeks of implementing this action plan, he had his first serious prospect meeting.

4. Alignment: Live Your Authentic Journey

As you embrace your authentic self and let go of societal expectations that don't serve you, you'll notice the noise of comparison fading into the background. When you're in alignment with your true self, you no longer feel the need to measure yourself against others because you're too busy living your own truth. Take a moment to envision and describe what this alignment feels like to you. This vision can serve as a powerful motivator on your journey.

Research in positive psychology shows that people who pursue goals aligned with their intrinsic values and authentic interests report greater fulfillment and sustainable motivation compared to those pursuing extrinsically motivated goals based on comparison or others' expectations.[11]

Tim's transformation was complete when he reached alignment. Instead of trying to emulate other consultants, he recognized his unique strengths in simplifying complex marketing challenges and building genuine relationships. He redesigned his services around these authentic gifts rather than trying to offer everything his competitors did. The result? Not only did he secure three clients, but they were ideal clients who valued exactly what he naturally excelled at. As Tim told me in our final session, "For the first time in my career, I feel like I'm succeeding as myself, not as some version of myself I thought I should be."

Try This:

- Regularly ask yourself, "If no one could judge me, what would I choose?"
- Seek out communities and relationships that celebrate your authentic self rather than fostering comparison

The goal isn't to never compare yourself to others—that's nearly impossible in our interconnected world. The goal is to build a strong enough sense of self that when comparisons do arise, they don't shake your foundation. You can observe them, learn from them if there's something valuable to glean, and then let them go without allowing them to define your worth or dictate your path.

From Comparison to Authentic Confidence

By implementing these strategies and consistently working on your self-awareness and self-compassion, you can gradually break free from the comparison trap. It's a journey, not a destination, and there will be ups and downs along the way. But with each step, you're reclaiming your power, honoring your individuality, and creating a life that's authentically yours.

What emerges when you release comparison isn't just the absence of a negative pattern—it's the presence of something beautiful: authentic confidence. Unlike confidence built on external validation or favorable comparisons, authentic confidence comes from within. It's stable, resilient, and reflects your true nature rather than a carefully constructed image.

This kind of confidence doesn't require you to be better than anyone else. It simply requires you to be fully, unapologetically yourself. And paradoxically, when you stop trying to measure up to others, you often find that your natural gifts and contributions shine even more brightly.

Key Takeaways:

- Comparison is a natural human tendency, but when unchecked, it becomes a major barrier to confidence and fulfillment
- Your unique path cannot be meaningfully compared to anyone else's journey
- Authentic confidence emerges when you release the need to measure yourself against others

- Self-compassion is more effective than self-criticism for building genuine confidence
- Creating boundaries around comparison triggers (like social media) can significantly improve well-being
- True confidence comes from living in alignment with your authentic self, not from favorable comparisons
- Perfectionism and imposter syndrome are often symptoms of an underlying comparison mindset
- Taking imperfect action is often the fastest way to build authentic confidence

Expert Insights on Comparison and Confidence

"Comparison is the thief of joy." — *Theodore Roosevelt*, whose observation on the destructive nature of comparison remains as relevant today as it was in his time.[12]

"The reason why we struggle with insecurity is because we compare our behind-the-scenes with everyone else's highlight reel." — Steven Furtick, whose work on confidence highlights how social media distorts our perception of others' lives.[13]

"Authenticity is the daily practice of letting go of who we think we're supposed to be and embracing who we are." — Brené Brown, whose research on vulnerability and courage has transformed our understanding of authentic confidence.[14]

"The privilege of a lifetime is being who you are." — Joseph Campbell, whose work on the hero's journey emphasizes the importance of following your own path rather than imitating others.[15]

Your Turn: Reflective Free Writing

Take a few minutes now to explore your relationship with comparison and authentic confidence.

Free Writing Prompts:

- When do I most often fall into the comparison trap? What triggers this pattern for me?
- If I were completely free from comparing myself to others, how would my life be different? What would I do, say, or pursue?
- What parts of my authentic self have I been hiding or downplaying because they don't measure up to others' expectations?
- What is one area where I can commit to defining success on my own terms rather than society's standards?

Unlocking Trust in Your Dreams

"Faith is taking the first step even when you don't see the whole staircase."

— *Martin Luther King Jr.*

W hen I was 33, my life seemed to be unfolding according to plan. Brian and I had been married for eight years and were proud parents to two wonderful boys. We had decided that two kids made for the perfect family size, neat and tidy. But deep within me, a persistent feeling stirred—like an unfinished sentence in a paragraph. I couldn't shake the vivid image of a family portrait with space for one more child.

Brian was content with our family of four. "Two kids are perfect, Laura," he'd insist. "Everything is better in even numbers." While I understood his perspective, the future I envisioned was unyielding. I felt it in my bones—this third child was waiting for us.

For nine months—ironically, the length of a full-term pregnancy—I worked on convincing Brian. Finally, he relented with a sigh, "Alright, Laura, I trust you." Trust—such a small word, yet so powerful in its meaning. I was thrilled but also terrified. Had I pressured him into this decision?

When we tried for our third child, it happened almost instantly, just as I had visualized. Less than a year later Charlie, our third son, completed our family portrait. But even amid this joy, doubt nagged at me. What if I had been wrong? What if Brian resented me for pushing for this change? It was a lesson in trusting my inner voice and letting go of the doubter within.

> **Reflection Moment:** Think about a time when your intuition was strongly guiding you toward something, even when logic or others suggested otherwise. Did you follow that inner knowing? What happened when you did (or didn't)?

Around the same time, another revelation struck me. While driving through an area we liked, a huge empty lot caught my eye. It was the largest lot in the neighborhood, with a backyard big enough for both a football and soccer field. We had just moved into a new home two years prior, and moving again seemed impractical. Yet, I couldn't shake the feeling that we were meant to be in this other neighborhood.

Brian was initially skeptical. "Can we afford it?" he asked. But just as with our third son Charlie, I knew this was part of our life story. I had some large commissions coming in from placements I'd made, and I was confident our finances would align. Brian took another leap of faith, echoing his earlier words: "I trust you, Laura."

We secured the lot that day, amid competition. The decision was swift but never rash; it was fueled by a vision so clear it left no room for doubt. Or at least, that's what I told myself. In reality, as we signed the papers and committed to this new path, I could feel the doubter in me stirring. What if I was wrong? What if I was leading our family into financial ruin? It took every ounce of my strength to silence that voice, to trust in my instincts.

We moved into our new home four weeks before Charlie was born. Our street brimmed with families, almost all with boys around the same age as ours. It was serendipity manifested, all because I dared to believe in a future that was initially invisible to others, including my husband. Today we vacation with our neighbors who have become some of our very best friends, friends we didn't know existed if we hadn't fully trusted in where we were being led.

Spiritual trust goes beyond trusting ourselves or others. It's about trusting in a higher purpose, a divine plan that often unfolds in ways we can't always understand or predict. It's about having faith that even when things don't make logical sense, there's a greater wisdom at play, and our job is to trust.

Research in neuroscience and psychology provides fascinating insights into how trust and belief influence our ability to create our desired reality. When we trust in our dreams and visions, we activate what neuroscientists call the "reticular activating system" (RAS)—a bundle of neurons in our brainstem that filters information based on what we focus on.[1]

This explains why, when you're considering buying a specific car model, you suddenly start seeing that model everywhere. Your RAS has been programmed to notice what aligns with your focus. Similarly, when you trust in a specific vision for your life, your brain naturally begins to filter for opportunities, connections, and pathways that support that vision.

Studies in the field of psychoneuroimmunology further demonstrate that positive expectation and belief (essential components of trust) create measurable changes in our nervous system, immune function, and even gene expression.[2] Our bodies literally begin to organize around what we deeply trust will happen, creating a biological environment conducive to manifesting those expectations.

Today, my eyes are set on a new vision. I see a platform—a show, a podcast, live events. Different from the events I hold today for marketing professionals (I started a business in 2018 connecting marketers via events, trainings and peer groups), this new vision is one where I get to impact thousands, perhaps even millions, of lives. I see a microphone and a camera. I see an audience being taken on an emotional roller coaster of joy, healing, inspiration, and empowerment. I am confident this or something better will come to pass, and I'm open to the signs as they're presented to me.

Yes, my aspirations are big, but I know that great things often have humble beginnings. Even if my first event has an audience of two, it will be a meaningful experience. Those two could be catalysts for something more significant. You never know where small steps will lead you. Don't be afraid to start small.

What's important to note is that even as I write these words, the battle rages within. I can feel the doubter in me starting to rise. Who am I to think I can have such an impact? What if I fail? What if no one cares about what I have to say? The voice of fear is always lurking, whispering its what-ifs. But I've come to realize that doubt is part of the human experience—even the most accomplished, inspiring people still wrestle with it. The key isn't eliminating doubt. It's learning to move forward despite it.

So as you step into your own big dreams, remember this: doubt is normal. It doesn't mean you're on the wrong path—it means you're stretching, growing, expanding beyond old limitations.

FEATURED PRACTICE: The Doubt Dialogue

When doubt arises about your dreams or intuitive guidance, try this powerful practice:

1. **Name the doubt**: Write down exactly what your inner doubter is saying. Be specific: "I'm afraid no one will attend my event" or "I doubt I can afford this move."
2. **Thank the doubter**: Acknowledge this part of you is trying to keep you safe. "Thank you for trying to protect me."

3. **Ask for evidence**: Write down: "What evidence do I have that this doubt is true?" and "What evidence do I have that the opposite might be true?"

4. **Connect with your deeper knowing**: Close your eyes, place a hand on your heart, and ask: "Beyond this doubt, what do I know to be true about this situation?"

5. **Choose your next step**: Based on this dialogue, decide on one small action that honors both your caution and your vision.

Research in cognitive psychology shows that externalizing our doubts through writing reduces their emotional impact and allows us to engage with them more objectively.[3] This practice doesn't eliminate doubt, but transforms your relationship with it, allowing you to move forward with both wisdom and courage.

The Neuroscience of Belief and Manifestation

My beliefs are heavily influenced by Dr. Wayne Dyer and Dr. Joe Dispenza, both masters in the art of manifesting reality.

Dyer taught me the importance of internal visualization— the idea that you must believe it to see it. Dr. Dispenza takes it further, blending neuroscience, quantum physics, and meditation to show how vividly experiencing something in your mind paves the neural pathways for it to come into your reality.

Their teachings mesmerized me, but more importantly, I put them into practice.

I am living proof that the mind can be rewired. When I catch a limiting thought—I'm not good enough—I don't let it spiral. I replace it with an empowering truth: "I am authentically me, and I am more than enough."

At first, it feels forced. Fake, even. But over time, repetition transforms belief. And when you change your thoughts, you change your life.

Dr. Dispenza's research shows that our brains cannot differentiate between a vividly imagined experience and a real one.[4] When we repeatedly imagine ourselves living our dreams with sensory richness and emotional intensity, our brains form new neural pathways as if we were actually having those experiences. This "mental rehearsal" creates neurological patterns that make our desired reality more likely to manifest.

And then there's money. The ever-present hurdle. The resistance that seems to stand between dreams and reality. But here's the truth: money is energy. If we can intentionally create thoughts that attract incredible experiences, why not do the same with abundance?

Joseph Campbell put it perfectly: "Money is congealed energy, and releasing it releases life's possibilities."

Think about that. Take out a dollar bill and hold it in your hand. Imagine where it's been, where it's going, the energy it carries.

How you do money is how you do life. Your relationship with money is a metaphor for your relationship with all energy—time, creativity, joy, even love.

I inherited my money story from my parents, who inherited theirs from their parents, who inherited theirs from their parents. Generations of beliefs passed down—beliefs about struggle, sacrifice, and the idea that wealth requires hardship. It took me years to unravel these patterns, but I finally arrived at a new truth: Money can come easily and effortlessly. I can offer my gifts in exchange for wealth. I can work fewer hours and earn abundantly. Money flows freely to me.

These weren't instant shifts. It took practice. But today, as I write these words, I believe them with 100% certainty.

What about you? What's your money story?

Think about the messages you absorbed growing up:
- Money doesn't grow on trees.
- You can't be wealthy and spiritual.
- Money is the root of all evil.

Now, challenge them. Because you get to decide what money means to you. If you want to go deeper, I highly recommend Maria Nemeth's The Energy of Money book.

I started rewriting my money story in 2016. At first, it felt unnatural. But today, I know in my bones: Money is not a struggle. Money comes to me effortlessly and easily when I'm in full alignment with myself.

And you know what? When you love money, it loves you back.

Research in behavioral economics and psychology confirms that our beliefs about money significantly impact our financial outcomes. Studies show that people with positive money mindsets earn more, save more, and report less financial stress than those with negative money beliefs, even when controlling for socioeconomic factors.[5]

> **Reflection Moment:** What beliefs about money did you inherit from your family? How might these beliefs be limiting your ability to trust in the financial aspect of your dreams? What new money story would better serve your vision?

Creating Your Future Now: The Power of Declaration

Dr. Dispenza teaches that when you vividly imagine your future, your brain and body work unconsciously to bring it to life.

So here it goes—my preview of what's to come:

- I am a $50K keynote speaker.
- I have created and invested in businesses that create *thousands* of meaningful jobs.
- I have a show and a conference that inspires millions of people worldwide.

These are not fantasies. They are events that will unfold in my reality. I see them in my mind's eye so clearly. It's this or something better.

Your thoughts shape your world. Choose them wisely. Choose them boldly. Choose them with intention.

Because the life you desire? It's already waiting for you to claim it.

The 4 A's Framework for Unlocking Trust

In the course of unlocking trust, the four integral A's - Awareness, Attitude, Action, and Alignment - can guide you:

1. Awareness: Recognize Your Mind's Power

Sharpen your mind's extraordinary power, particularly in visualization, to bring your goals to fruition. Consider a daily mindfulness practice—start with just 5 minutes every morning meditating or journaling. Research shows that such practices can cultivate acute self-awareness. Take this a step further by creating a vision board, a practice correlated with goal achievement. But as you practice awareness, be conscious of the doubter within you. Acknowledge its presence, see it, feel it. Write it down. Breathe through it. Your heightened level of awareness allows you to see and feel. If we cannot see, feel, and acknowledge the doubts, how can we expect to overcome them?

Studies in cognitive neuroscience confirm that visualization activates many of the same neural networks involved in actually performing or experiencing what we visualize.[6] When we consistently visualize our desired future, we're essentially training our brains to recognize and create the conditions for that future to manifest.

Try This:

- Create a detailed sensory vision of your dream life—what do you see, hear, feel, taste, and smell in this vision?
- Practice 5 minutes of visualization each morning, immersing yourself fully in the experience of your dream already achieved
- Keep a "doubt journal" where you record your doubts without judgment, creating awareness of your thought patterns

2. Attitude: Cultivate Possibility Thinking

Cultivate a mindset that supports your vision and dreams. It's about shifting from "I can't" to "I can," from "it's impossible" to "how can this happen?" Develop an attitude of curiosity and possibility. When doubts arise, instead of letting them derail you, ask yourself, "What if this works out even better than I imagined?" This shift in attitude can be the difference between giving up and pushing through challenges.

Psychologist Carol Dweck's groundbreaking research on growth mindset shows that people who believe their abilities can be developed through dedication and action (rather than being fixed traits) are more likely to achieve their goals and bounce back from setbacks.[7] A growth mindset is essential for maintaining trust in your dreams through inevitable challenges.

FEATURED PRACTICE:
The Possibility Question

When facing a challenge or doubt about your dream, transform your thinking with this practice:

1. **Notice limitation thinking**: Identify when you're thinking in terms of limitations ("This is impossible" or "I can't figure this out").
2. **Pause and breathe**: Take three deep breaths to interrupt the limitation pattern.
3. **Ask possibility questions**: Replace limiting thoughts with questions that open possibilities:

   ○ "What if this could work out better than I imagined?"
   ○ "How might this challenge be preparing me for something greater?"
   ○ "If anything were possible, what would my next step be?"
   ○ "Who could help me see new possibilities I haven't considered?"

4. **Capture insights**: Write down any insights or ideas that emerge.

> Research shows that the questions we ask ourselves
> directly shape our perception and cognitive processing.
> By asking possibility-oriented questions rather than
> dwelling on limitations, we activate the brain's problem-
> solving capacity and creative thinking.[8]

3. Action: Move Forward Despite Doubt

Visualization is powerful, but concrete steps must follow your
ambitions. Break your grand vision into actionable steps, each
with a realistic deadline. Take action every single day, even as
small as it might be.

Studies in behavioral psychology reveal that action itself can
generate motivation and confidence, rather than the other way
around.[9] We often believe we need to feel confident before acting,
but research shows that taking action—even small steps—builds
the very confidence and trust we're seeking.

Try This:

- Identify one small action you can take today toward a dream
  in your heart
- Break your vision into 90-day action plans with specific,
  measurable steps
- Celebrate each action taken, regardless of outcome, reinforcing
  your identity as someone who moves forward despite doubt

4. Alignment: Connect Actions with Core Values

Ensure your actions resonate with your core values and beliefs. It's not uncommon for projects or visions to start with enthusiasm but eventually fizzle out. This often happens due to a misalignment between one's actions and core values. If what you're doing doesn't resonate at a deep, fundamental level, maintaining momentum becomes a struggle. Therefore, scrutinize your "why" and validate its compatibility with your values and beliefs. When your actions, big or small, align with your deeply held beliefs and values, the likelihood of your vision coming to fruition increases exponentially.

By shifting your focus to aligning your deepest "why," core values, and foundational beliefs, you create an unbreakable chain that ties your daily actions to your ultimate goals. You replace self-doubt with self-assurance. The doubter within you will always try to pull you off course. It's up to you to keep realigning, to keep trusting in yourself and your vision. With awareness, the right attitude, and aligned action, you can and will stay on track.

Research on intrinsic motivation demonstrates that people are more likely to persist toward goals that connect with their core values and sense of purpose, even when facing significant obstacles.[10] This alignment creates a sustainable source of energy and commitment that external motivators cannot match.

Try This:

- Write your personal mission statement that connects your dreams to your deepest values (see the end of this chapter for how to do this)
- For each action in your plan, identify how it aligns with your core values
- Regularly review and refine your goals to ensure they remain aligned with your values

"Believe it to see it" isn't just an inspirational phrase; it's a roadmap. A roadmap that guides you through the intricate process of turning what you believe into a reality you can see, touch, and experience. But that roadmap is useless if you don't trust in your ability to follow it. If you let the doubter within you steer you off course.

It all starts with a single belief. With belief, you can see your future; without it, you're walking through life blindfolded. But belief alone isn't enough. You must trust yourself. You must trust in your gifts. You must trust in your vision. And most importantly, let go of the doubter within you that tries to hold you back.

To build this trust, start small. Set a small, achievable goal and follow through. Each time you do this, you're building trust in yourself. You're proving to yourself that you can do what you set out to do. Over time, these small wins accumulate, building a foundation of self-trust that can weather any storm of doubt.

Don't forget to practice self-compassion. When doubts arise or things don't go as planned, treat yourself with kindness. Speak to yourself as you would to a dear friend facing a challenge. This self-compassion builds a sense of safety and security, making it easier to trust yourself and take risks.

Also be sure to surround yourself with supportive people who believe in you and your vision. Their trust in you can help bolster your own self-trust, especially in moments of doubt. But remember, while external support is valuable, the most important trust is the trust you have in yourself, your gifts, and your worthiness.

Be sure to regularly revisit and celebrate your successes, no matter how small. Keep a "win journal" where you record your achievements. In moments of doubt, review this journal to remind yourself of your capabilities and the times you've overcome challenges.

Finally, remember that trust is not about being certain of the outcome. It's about being certain of your ability to handle whatever comes your way. It's about knowing that no matter what happens, you have the resilience, creativity, and strength to navigate it. It's about your trust in your ability to figure things out. You have before, and you'll do it again.

Choose to see. Choose to believe. Choose to trust. Because when you do, there's no limit to what you can achieve. The path may not always be clear, and doubts may arise, but with trust in yourself and your vision, you have the power to create the life and impact you dream of. Your journey of unlocking trust is not just about achieving your goals; it's about becoming the person who is capable of achieving those goals. And that person is already within you, waiting to be trusted, waiting to shine.

Key Takeaways:

- Trusting your intuitive wisdom is essential for creating a life aligned with your deepest purpose
- The battle between vision and doubt is normal—even the most successful people experience it
- Your beliefs about what's possible directly impact your brain's ability to create that reality
- Money beliefs can either limit or expand your capacity to manifest abundance
- Small wins build self-trust that creates momentum toward bigger achievements
- Trust is less about certainty in outcomes and more about confidence in your ability to navigate challenges
- Visualization paired with aligned action creates powerful pathways for manifesting your dreams

Expert Insights on Trust

"You'll see it when you believe it." — Dr. Wayne Dyer, whose research on intention and manifestation has helped millions understand the relationship between belief and physical reality.[11]

"When you change the way you look at things, the things you look at change." — Dr. Max Planck, Nobel Prize-winning physicist whose work in quantum theory revealed how observation influences physical reality.[12]

"Your brain doesn't know the difference between what's happening out there and what's happening in here." — Dr. Joe Dispenza, whose research combines neuroscience and quantum physics to explain how mental rehearsal creates neurological changes.[13]

"The best way to predict your future is to create it." — Abraham Lincoln, whose life exemplified the power of vision and persistence despite numerous setbacks and challenges.[14]

Your Turn: Your Personal Mission Statement

A personal mission statement is different from a goal list. Goals are destinations; a mission statement is your internal compass that guides every decision, every action, and ultimately shapes who you become. When your deepest values align with your biggest dreams, you create unstoppable momentum.

Let's go through this process step by step. Give yourself the gift of uninterrupted time. Find a quiet space where you can think deeply and feel fully. This journey inward deserves your complete presence.

Step 1: Dream Activation

Before we can connect your dreams to your values, let's clarify those dreams. Close your eyes and imagine yourself five years from now, living a life that would make you proud. What are you doing? Who are you with? How do you feel? Don't censor yourself or worry about practicality yet.

In your journal, answer these questions:

- What achievements would make you feel your life has been meaningful?
- What would you attempt if you knew you couldn't fail?
- What activities make you lose track of time?
- What legacy do you want to leave in your career and life?

Step 2: Values Excavation

Now, let's uncover your core values – these are the principles that matter most to you, that you're unwilling to compromise.

Consider these prompts:

- Think of a time when you felt most alive, proud, and fulfilled. What values were you honoring in that moment?
- What injustices or situations make you feel angry or frustrated? (These often point to violated values)
- If you could instill just three values in a child, what would they be?
- What qualities do you most admire in others?

Circle the 5-7 values that resonate most deeply. These might include integrity, creativity, freedom, service, growth, connection, excellence, or others unique to you.

Step 3: Bridge Building

This is where the magic happens. We're going to build the bridge between your dreams and your values.

For each of your top values, ask:

- How does this value support my dreams?
- How might my dreams allow me to express this value more fully?
- Are there any dreams that conflict with my core values? If so, how might I reimagine those dreams?

The strongest missions emerge when your values fuel your dreams and your dreams express your values.

Step 4: Crafting Your Statement

Now, craft your personal mission statement. This isn't about perfection–it's about authentic expression. Your statement might be a paragraph, a few sentences, or even a powerful phrase.

Consider this framework: "I will [how you'll express your values] in order to [what dreams you'll pursue] so that [the impact you want to create]."

For example: "I will lead with courage and compassion in developing innovative healthcare solutions that empower people to take control of their wellbeing and live more vibrant lives."

Or: "My mission is to use my creativity and perseverance to build businesses that solve meaningful problems while creating opportunities for others to thrive."

Step 5: Living Your Mission

Your mission statement isn't meant to sit in your journal gathering dust. It's meant to be lived. Consider these ways to integrate it:

- Read it aloud each morning to set your intention for the day
- Review it before making significant decisions
- Share it with trusted people who can support you and hold you accountable
- Revisit and refine it quarterly as you grow and evolve

Remember, a personal mission statement is a living document. As you change and grow, it may evolve too. What matters is that it continues to connect your deepest values with your most meaningful dreams.

CHAPTER

Unlocking Action

"What you do makes a difference, and you have to decide what kind of difference you want to make."

— *Jane Goodall*

hen we think of life-changing moments, we often imagine dramatic transformations—major breakthroughs, pivotal decisions, or unexpected revelations. But what if the most profound shifts don't come from grand gestures, but from the smallest, most intentional actions? What if a single choice, a subtle shift in how we engage with others, had the power to change everything?

I've noticed that the most magnetic, joy-filled people are those who show genuine interest in others. There's something powerful about someone who not only asks thoughtful questions but also follows through with meaningful actions. I once had a friend who embodied this beautifully—she didn't just listen, she acted. After our conversations, she would surprise me with a book related to something we discussed or send a handwritten card in the mail with words that spoke directly to my heart. She wasn't just making me feel seen and valued—she was demonstrating, through her actions, what true connection looks like.

That realization transformed how I moved through life.

I used to wake up feeling like I was simply going through the motions. Now, I wake up excited, wondering who I'll meet, what I'll learn, and how I can show up for the people crossing my path. Every encounter holds a lesson, a message, or even a hidden blessing—but unlocking that treasure requires curiosity. It means being intentional, not only in starting conversations but in acting on what I learn.

> **Reflection Moment:** Think about someone who makes you feel truly seen and valued. What specific actions do they take that create that feeling? How might you incorporate similar actions into your own interactions?

I began taking aligned action every time someone touched my soul. At first, it was as simple as sending an email or a handwritten note. Now, it's a voice memo or a spontaneous text when someone crosses my mind—not just on their birthday like everyone else, but in the in-between moments when they least expect it.

Because here's the truth: We learn so much about ourselves through others, but it's what we do with that knowledge that leaves a lasting impact.

This is where the power of action comes into play. It's not enough to listen, to understand, or even to empathize. The real magic happens when we take what we've learned and turn it into something tangible—something that lifts, supports, and reminds others that they matter.

In today's world, active listening is a lost art. But even more rare? The initiative to act on what we hear.

We text instead of talk. Swipe instead of connect. Engage, but rarely follow through.

But real connection? It's more than just listening. It's watching, observing, and being genuinely curious. And most of all, it's about turning those moments of connection into meaningful action—because that's where relationships deepen, impact grows, and life truly begins to change.

The Science of Action and Connection

Research in social psychology has consistently shown that what we do matters more than what we say when it comes to building trust and connection. Studies reveal that follow-through actions create what scientists call "behavioral integrity"—the alignment between words and deeds that forms the foundation of trust in relationships.[1]

What's particularly fascinating is how even micro-actions can have macro impacts on well-being. A study published in the Journal of Happiness Studies found that performing small acts of kindness led to significant increases in life satisfaction and positive emotions for the giver.[2] These benefits weren't dependent on the size of the action but rather on its authenticity and intentionality.

Neuroscience offers additional insights into why action matters so much for our relationships. When someone follows through on something they've learned about us, our brains release oxytocin—often called the "bonding hormone"—creating a neural foundation for deeper connection.[3] This helps explain why thoughtful actions can create such powerful impressions in our relationships, often more lasting than words alone.

FEATURED PRACTICE: The Connection Action Plan

Transform your relationships through intentional follow-through using this simple practice:

1. **Listen actively**: During your next three conversations, focus completely on the other person. Note one specific need, interest, or challenge they mention (even if they don't directly ask for help).
2. **Plan one action**: For each person, identify one small, specific action you could take related to what you learned—sending an article, offering assistance with a task, or simply acknowledging a feeling.
3. **Act within 48 hours**: The timing of your action matters. Research shows that follow-through within 48 hours creates the strongest impression of authenticity and care.
4. **Focus on quality, not recognition**: Take the action without expectation of acknowledgment or reciprocation. The goal is genuine service, not credit.

5. **Notice the impact**: Pay attention to how taking this action affects both the recipient and you. What shifts in the relationship? How do you feel afterward?

Studies conducted by Dr. John Gottman, relationship researcher at the University of Washington, found that responding to others' "bids for connection" (like the needs or interests they share in conversation) with action rather than just acknowledgment predicted relationship success with 80% accuracy.[4]

Remember during the pandemic when everyone was wearing masks? Even with faces covered, you could still feel a smile. It was in the crinkle of someone's eyes, the warmth in their gaze. I made it a point not only to smile beneath my mask but to make intentional eye contact with people—at the grocery store, at the gas station, anywhere I could.

Sometimes, I would silently say to myself, I bless you. I see you. And then, I'd look for a way to turn that blessing into action—helping someone reach an item on a high shelf, letting a rushed shopper go ahead of me in line, or simply offering an extra moment of kindness. These small, intentional acts changed me as much as I hope they impacted others.

I've learned that genuine curiosity, asking meaningful questions, and then acting on what you learn creates a ripple effect. It tells someone, I am here with you. You matter. And when people feel seen in that way, something shifts—it fosters a connection deeper than words, one that surprises and uplifts both people involved.

Have you ever stopped to really wonder about someone's life, and then taken an extra step to make their day a little brighter?

This is where action meets intention. It's one thing to feel for someone—to empathize with their struggles or frustrations. But it's another thing entirely to do something about it.

Transforming Difficult Relationships Through Action

Take, for example, that neighbor. You know the one. We all have (or have had) that neighbor—the chronic complainer, the one who drains the energy from a conversation before it even begins. I had a real doozy of one in the past.

Instead of avoiding her, like I might have in years past, I challenged myself to shift the dynamic. What if I could change the emotional climate of our interactions? What if, instead of absorbing her negativity, I could be the one to bring light into the space?

So I experimented.

I began steering our conversations toward more positive topics. I listened for moments where I could offer genuine encouragement. And beyond words, I started doing—bringing small gifts, offering to help with tasks she mentioned, looking for ways to bring warmth where there had been only frustration.

At first, it was just an act of kindness. But then, something deeper emerged.

By choosing to show up with love, I started to see myself more clearly.

I realized that what triggered me about my neighbor wasn't just her negativity—it was the way I allowed myself to shut down in response to it. She became a mirror, revealing parts of myself that still needed healing.

Through this practice, I wasn't just offering love to her—I was learning to love myself in a new way. And that's the real magic of taking action. It's not just about lifting others. It's about lifting yourself in the process.

Because the way we treat others is often a reflection of how we treat ourselves. And when we start making kindness, love, and intentional action a habit, the world around us begins to shift in ways we never expected.

> **Reflection Moment:** Think about a challenging relationship in your life. What specific actions could you take to shift the dynamic, regardless of how the other person responds? How might these actions change not just the relationship, but your own perspectives and patterns?

In the end, every act of genuine interest, every moment of active listening, and every follow-through action contributes to a ripple effect. It's about modeling a behavior you'd like to see in the world. Even if you can't be all things to all people, you can choose where your focus and your efforts go. By shifting from a 'me-centric' to an 'other-centric' approach and backing it up with action, not only do we enrich our lives, but we also open the door for others to do the same.

If you're wondering whether a simple action can truly change lives, consider this: A study by the American Psychological Association found that people with strong social connections tend to be happier, healthier, and live longer. But these connections aren't built on words alone; they're built on actions that demonstrate genuine care.

Imagine being in a relationship where you feel constantly misunderstood, where your partner hears your words but never acts on them. The emotional toll can be devastating. However, when both parties take the time to not only genuinely listen to each other—to understand the fears, the dreams, the quirks—but also to act on that understanding, the relationship transforms. It becomes a safe space where both individuals can grow and thrive. This is the power of action in our personal relationships.

Action in Leadership: The CEO's Circle Talks

Now let's pivot to professional settings. Many organizations are plagued by low employee engagement, high turnover rates, and a lack of innovation. These issues can often be traced back to a lack of genuine connection and follow-through action. I get to talk to many job seekers who confide in me the real reason they're looking for a new job: most don't feel valued by their leader, and this is often demonstrated not just in words but in a lack of action.

I worked with a CEO who understood the importance of not only having meaningful conversations but also taking meaningful actions. Once a month, he would host what he called "Circle Talks" with his team, where everyone could speak openly about their concerns, ideas, or even personal triumphs and struggles. But he didn't stop there. He would take the insights from these talks and use them to drive real change in the organization, whether it was implementing a new policy, providing additional resources, or even just following up with a personal note of encouragement.

The impact on employee morale and productivity was palpable. It didn't just change the conversation; it changed the culture. As people began to feel heard and valued, and saw their input leading to tangible actions, the work environment became more positive, cooperative, and innovative. It was a genuine leader who wanted the truth and was willing to act on it, even if the truth stung every once in a while. Wouldn't you rather know the truth and have the chance to act on it than pretend you think you know how everyone is doing?

Action is what separates great leaders from good ones. It's not enough to listen, nod in agreement, or say the right things. True leadership, true impact, comes from taking deliberate, meaningful action based on what you've learned.

Leadership research confirms this pattern. A comprehensive study of employee engagement by Gallup found that employees who felt their feedback led to visible action were 4.6 times more likely to feel empowered to do their best work.[5] The most effective leaders don't just collect insights—they convert them into tangible changes that demonstrate genuine care for their team's concerns.

So, what is one small step you can take right now to move closer to your goal? Pause and identify it. Maybe it's sending that email, making that call, or blocking time for a project that truly matters to you. Take that step today—no matter how small it seems. Because action, no matter how minor, creates momentum.

But here's the key: genuine action matters more than just "doing." This isn't about checking off a box or performing kindness because it's expected. The most powerful actions come from a place of sincerity—when they bring you joy, when they stem from love, care, and a true desire to uplift others. When you act from this authentic place, your actions carry greater weight, create deeper impact, and leave a lasting imprint—not just on others, but on you as well.

Try This:

- Identify one action you've been postponing and commit to taking the first small step within 24 hours
- Each morning, ask yourself: "What's one meaningful action I can take today that aligns with my values?"
- At the end of each day, reflect on what you did, not just what you thought about or planned

Let me be crystal clear about something: this step—taking action—is absolutely critical to becoming the person you want to be. You don't make progress by just thinking about your dreams; you make progress by doing.

When I first started my coaching business, do you think I had it all figured out? Not even close! I've gone through about 20 different iterations of my coaching packages, and they're still evolving to this day. If I had waited until everything was "perfect" before launching, I'd still be sitting on the sidelines, endlessly planning but never growing.

I was not confident in myself by any means. I messed up—a lot. I set my prices too low, then too high. I over delivered to the point of exhaustion, then had to recalibrate. I created programs that didn't quite land, then refined them based on feedback. Each "failure" wasn't really a failure at all—it was valuable data that could only come through action.

Here's the truth that changed everything for me: you've got to have grace for yourself just like you have grace for others. And just know, you are going to do it scared if it's something you've never done before.

I'll never forget my first keynote speech to a room of 150 people. Despite practicing that speech over 50 times in preparation, I was literally shaking when I took the mic. My voice trembled for the first few minutes. But I kept going, and something magical happened—I found my rhythm, connected with the audience, and delivered a talk that received a standing ovation.

That moment taught me something I'll never forget: people will praise you in public for what you practice in private. It took putting in the reps. No one saw the 50 practice sessions in my living room. No one knew how many times I rewrote that speech or how many hours I spent rehearsing my delivery. They only saw the result.

So whatever is calling you forward—whether it's starting a business, writing a book, having a difficult conversation, or making a major life change—begin putting in the reps. Take imperfect action. Start before you feel ready, because honestly, you may never feel 100% ready for the things that matter most.

Action builds confidence—not the other way around. Don't wait to feel confident before you begin; begin, and watch your confidence grow with each step, each rep, each lesson learned through doing.

In the context of taking action, the Law of Reciprocity can create a beautiful cycle of positive interactions. When you take genuine action to help or support someone, they're likely to feel a natural inclination to reciprocate, either to you directly or by paying it forward to someone else. This creates a chain reaction of kindness and positive actions that can transform communities and relationships.

Consider the old adage, "Treat others as you want to be treated." This golden rule takes on new significance when we think about it in terms of action. Imagine if you were ever in need, whether facing a visible challenge like a physical ailment that limits your capabilities, or battling an invisible struggle like emotional drain or depression. In those moments, wouldn't a genuine action to help make all the difference?

I remember a time when I was going through a particularly difficult period. I was dealing with overwhelming anxiety and feeling isolated. A friend noticed something was off, even though I hadn't said anything. Instead of asking me if I was okay and leaving it at that, she took action. She showed up at my door with flowers and chocolate and simply said, "I thought you might need some company." That simple act of kindness, that genuine action based on care and attention, meant the world to me. It helped me feel seen and supported when I needed it most.

Research in behavioral economics confirms this reciprocity effect. Studies show that receiving an unexpected act of kindness creates a psychological drive to "pay it forward" that can influence behavior for days afterward.[6] This creates what sociologists call "positive contagion," where helpful actions spread through social networks like a beneficial virus.

Authentic Action: Aligning Deeds with Your Unique Gifts

It's not about grand gestures or doing things because we feel obligated. It's about those sincere, often small actions that come from a place of real care and attention to others. By treating others with kindness and taking genuine action to support them, we're not only helping them in the moment, but we're also creating a support network for ourselves. We're contributing to a culture of care and action that we might one day need to lean on ourselves.

This approach to action also allows for more creativity and personal expression in how we choose to help or connect with others. Instead of following a script of what we think we "should" do, we can tap into our unique skills, interests, and perspectives to offer support in ways that are meaningful to us and impactful for others.

For example, if you're a great cook, you might show support by preparing meals for a friend going through a tough time. If you're a good listener, your action might be to create space for deep, meaningful conversations. If you're talented at organization, you might offer to help an overwhelmed colleague streamline their workspace or schedule.

By aligning our actions with our authentic selves and genuine desires to help, we're more likely to sustain our efforts over time. Actions that come from obligation or expectation can lead to burnout or resentment. But when we act from a place of authenticity and joy, we're energized by our actions. We create a positive feedback loop where our actions bring us joy, which inspires more positive action.

FEATURED PRACTICE:
The Signature Action Inventory

Discover your most authentic and energizing ways to take action with this exercise:

1. **List your gifts**: Write down 3-5 natural gifts or skills that come easily to you (e.g., listening, writing, organizing, cooking, problem-solving).
2. **Identify energy sources**: For each strength, note when using it gives you energy rather than depleting you. What conditions make this strength feel joyful to use?
3. **Create action categories**: Based on your energizing strengths, create a few "signature action categories" that feel authentic to you. Examples might include:

- ○ "Thoughtful written notes" (if writing energizes you)
- ○ "Organizational assistance" (if you love creating systems)
- ○ "Homemade meals" (if cooking brings you joy)
- ○ "Deep listening sessions" (if presence is your gift)

4. **Commit to authenticity**: When you identify a need or opportunity to help someone, choose actions from your signature categories rather than defaulting to conventional responses.

Research in positive psychology shows that actions aligned with our "character strengths" (our natural talents and values) create significantly greater wellbeing benefits than those that don't tap into our authentic gifts.[7]

The 4 A's Framework for Taking Meaningful Action

So, what can you do today? The 4 A's framework can be a game-changer when it comes to unlocking the ability and initiative to take action to shine brighter. Let's break it down:

1. Awareness: Notice Opportunities for Action

Start by being aware of the opportunities for meaningful action that surround you every day. Research by Dr. Elizabeth Stokoe, a conversation analyst, suggests that active listening can create a space for groundbreaking discussions, but it's what you do with that space that truly matters. So tune into the nuances, the emotions, and the unstated needs that may be subtly communicated when you converse with someone, and then consider how you can address those needs through action.

Dr. Stokoe's research reveals that what we hear in conversations is often just the tip of the iceberg.[8] Beneath explicit requests or statements lie deeper needs and desires that represent opportunities for meaningful action. By developing what psychologists call "conversational intelligence"—the ability to hear what's not being said—we can identify these action opportunities that others might miss.

Try This:

- Practice "listening beyond words" in your next three conversations, noting non-verbal cues and emotional undertones
- Keep an "action opportunity journal" where you record moments when you sensed someone needed support
- Ask open-ended follow-up questions that invite deeper sharing when you sense there's more beneath the surface

2. Attitude: Approach with Openness and Non-Judgment

Sometimes, we enter conversations with preconceived notions or judgments that prevent us from truly hearing what the other person is saying and, consequently, from taking meaningful action. Checking your attitude means approaching every interaction with an open mind, willing to consider perspectives different from your own and remind yourself that there's really not a right or wrong way, there's simply what is. We want to put labels on people, on groups, on what is right or wrong. In this stage, can we seek to understand rather than judge?

Research in cognitive science has identified what's called "confirmation bias"—our tendency to notice information that confirms our existing beliefs while filtering out contradictory evidence.[9] This bias can severely limit our ability to identify opportunities for meaningful action, especially with people who differ from us. Consciously adopting an attitude of openness and curiosity counteracts this bias.

Try This:

- Before important conversations, set an intention to learn something new about the other person
- Practice "perspective-taking" by imagining the situation from the other person's point of view
- When judgmental thoughts arise, note them without acting on them, and return to curiosity

3. Action: Move from Intention to Implementation

Once you're aware and adopt an attitude that who you are matters, the next step is the DO. Inspired action. Not dwelling in all the possible outcomes but knowing only good can come if you are coming from a place of love, a place of service, a place where you know your intentions. You don't need to get instant gratification from your actions. Rather, you need to know your actions are in alignment with who you are and who you aspire to be. How many times has someone said, "I'll follow up with you" and you never hear from them again? Don't be that person. Honor your commitments. Honor your word.

The gap between intention and action has been extensively studied by psychologists. Research on "implementation intentions"—specific plans that link situations to responses—shows that people who create concrete action plans are 2-3 times more likely to follow through than those with general intentions.[10] This explains why vague commitments like "I'll get in touch" rarely translate to action, while specific plans ("I'll email you the article by Tuesday") have a much higher completion rate.

Try This:

- Convert vague intentions into specific action commitments with clear timing
- Use the "if-then" planning method: "If X happens, then I will take Y specific action"

- Create accountability by sharing your action commitments with someone else

4. Alignment: Ensure Actions Reflect Your Values

Make sure that your participation in the conversation and your subsequent actions are not just surface-level; delve deep and align them with what truly matters to you and the other person involved. Dr. Brené Brown, a research professor at the University of Houston, emphasizes the importance of aligning your conversations and your actions with your values to achieve a more profound, meaningful connection and impact.

Dr. Brown's research reveals that when our actions align with our core values, we experience what she calls "wholehearted living"—a state of greater fulfillment, resilience, and authentic connection.[11] When we act in ways that contradict our deeper values, even small misalignments create what psychologists call "cognitive dissonance"—a state of mental discomfort that can lead to rationalization, avoidance, or diminished wellbeing.

Try This:

- Identify your top 3-5 core values and review your planned actions against this list
- Ask yourself: "If someone who shares my values saw this action, would they recognize it as an expression of those values?"

- Regularly reflect on your actions to assess whether they're creating the impact and relationships you truly desire

The emphasis on Action in this chapter is crucial because it's often the missing link between good intentions and real change. Many of us are aware of opportunities to make a difference. Many of us have the right attitude and want to help. But it's the step of taking action that often gets overlooked or postponed. This practice of aligned action aims to bridge that gap, to inspire you to move from thought to deed, from intention to impact.

You're only one conversation and one action away from someone changing your life—or you changing theirs. It's truly that simple. You don't need permission to make a change; you just need the courage to take the first step and the commitment to follow through.

So go ahead, lean in, listen, and most importantly, act. Let the transformation begin. Because remember, in the grand picture of life, it's not the big moments but the seemingly trivial conversations and small actions that make all the difference. And in that radiant light of genuine human connection and purposeful action, we find our most authentic selves shining brighter, one conversation and one deed at a time.

Key Takeaways:

- Small, intentional actions often create more profound impacts than grand gestures

- The gap between listening and action is where most connection opportunities are lost
- How you act matters more than what you say in building trust and meaningful relationships
- Every authentic action creates ripple effects that extend far beyond what you can see
- Your unique strengths determine your most authentic and energizing ways to take action
- Creating specific implementation plans dramatically increases follow-through on good intentions
- Actions aligned with your core values create sustainable positive impact for both others and yourself

Expert Insights on Action and Impact

"Never doubt that a small group of thoughtful, committed citizens can change the world; indeed, it's the only thing that ever has." — Margaret Mead, anthropologist whose research demonstrated how individual actions shape cultural transformation.[12]

"Do the best you can until you know better. Then when you know better, do better." — Maya Angelou, whose life's work embodied the connection between awareness and meaningful action.[13]

"Act as if what you do makes a difference. It does." — William James, pioneering psychologist whose research laid the groundwork for understanding how actions shape not only our external world but our internal experience.[14]

"In a gentle way, you can shake the world." — Mahatma Gandhi, whose philosophy of nonviolent action demonstrated how seemingly small, principled acts could create massive social change.[15]

Your Turn: Reflective Free Writing

Take a few minutes now to explore your relationship with meaningful action. Find a quiet space, set a timer for 10 minutes, and write continuously without editing or judging what comes up. You might consider these prompts:

Free Writing Prompts:

- When have you experienced the positive impact of someone taking meaningful action based on what they learned about you? How did it make you feel?
- What patterns do you notice in your own follow-through? Where do you consistently take action, and where do you tend to stop at good intentions?
- What small action have you been postponing that could make a significant difference in someone's life or in your own progress?
- If you committed to one small, meaningful action each day for the next month, how might your relationships and sense of purpose transform?

CHAPTER

Unlocking Your Authenticity

"The privilege of a lifetime is to become who you truly are."

— Carl Jung

I n a world swarming with demands and distractions, it's easy to lose ourselves in the pursuit of perfection. We strive to be the perfect employee, the perfect partner, the perfect friend, the perfect everything. But in this relentless chase, we often lose sight of our authentic selves. The one place where we need to be rooted, for the sake of our sanity and well-being, is in our own truth, our own reality, our own imperfect but beautiful existence.

Throughout the previous chapters, we've touched on the importance of authenticity in various aspects of our lives. Whether it's in finding joy in our work, trusting our intuition, or taking meaningful action, being true to ourselves has been an underlying theme. However, the journey to authenticity is so crucial and often challenging that it deserves a deeper exploration. It's the foundation upon which we build a fulfilling life, and understanding its nuances can be transformative.

> **Reflection Moment:** Think about a time when you felt you had to be "perfect" rather than authentic. How did it feel in your body? What was the cost of maintaining that facade? What would have changed if you had allowed yourself to be real in that moment?

An important step in my growth journey has been learning to embrace my authentic self, flaws and all. As someone deeply empathic, with a natural inclination to serve and help others, I often found myself stretched too thin, trying to be everything to everyone. I thought if I could just be perfect, if I could anticipate and meet every need, I would be worthy of love and acceptance. But this pursuit of perfection was not only detrimental to my well-being, but also bred resentment and emotional burnout.

It took several painful friendships (ok, and romantic relationships) for me to fully learn this lesson: just be you. Weird, quirky you. The ones that love you won't mind this quirky version of you. The ones that need you to be someone else, well guess what? I am no longer available for that. Eventually, my Laura-ness burst out and, in most cases, the friendship got way easier. Or it didn't and it ended. And that's okay. I've learned that being me was more important than molding into a fake me.

This realization was liberating, but it didn't come easy. It required a conscious effort to peel back the layers of who

I thought I should be and reveal who I truly am. It meant facing my fears of rejection and judgment, and choosing to be vulnerable anyway. But with each step towards authenticity, I found myself feeling more alive, more connected, and paradoxically, more accepted.

The Science of Authenticity

Research in psychology offers fascinating insights into why authenticity is so vital for our well-being. Studies show that people who live authentically report significantly higher levels of life satisfaction, self-esteem, and positive emotions, while experiencing less stress, anxiety, and depression.[1]

What's particularly interesting is how authenticity affects our relationships. When we present an authentic self to the world, we create what psychologists call "psychological safety"—an environment where genuine connection can flourish. This safety allows both ourselves and others to be vulnerable, leading to deeper, more meaningful relationships.[2]

Neuroscience research has found that maintaining a false self actually creates measurable stress in the brain and body. When we're inauthentic, the brain's conflict-monitoring systems activate, creating cognitive strain similar to what we experience when telling a lie.[3] This explains why maintaining a facade feels so exhausting—it literally taxes our neural resources.

FEATURED PRACTICE:
The Authenticity Check-In

Use this simple but powerful practice to reconnect with your authentic self when you feel pulled toward people-pleasing or perfectionism:

1. **Pause and breathe**: Take three deep breaths, placing a hand on your heart if possible.
2. **Body scan**: Notice how you feel physically. Where is there tension? Where is there ease? Your body often knows when you're betraying your authentic self.
3. **Ask yourself**: "If no one else's opinion mattered right now, what would I truly want to say/do/choose in this situation?"
4. **Find the middle path**: Consider what small step toward authenticity you could take that honors both your needs and the realities of the situation.
5. **Affirm your choice**: Whether you choose full authenticity or a small step in that direction, acknowledge your awareness—this itself is growth.

Research by Dr. Susan David of Harvard Medical School shows that this type of emotional awareness practice helps bridge the gap between our automated reactions (like people-pleasing) and our more authentic responses.[4] Even when external circumstances require some compromise, the simple act of checking in with your authentic self reduces internal conflict and builds self-trust.

Saying No to Grow

Embracing authenticity doesn't mean you cease to help or connect; it means you do so from a space of honesty and self-acceptance. It means being real about your capacities, your boundaries, and your needs. It means showing up as you are, not as you think you should be. This shift can be subtle but profound, affecting every aspect of your life.

I remember a pivotal moment in my early 30s when I was asked to take on a project at work that I knew would push me beyond my limits. In the past, I would have said yes without hesitation, driven by the need to prove my worth and be the perfect employee. But this time, something stopped me. It was a quiet but firm voice within me that said, "No, this is not for you. This will deplete you, not fulfill you."

It was a scary moment. I was afraid of disappointing my boss, being seen as incapable or unwilling. But I also knew that saying yes would mean betraying myself. So, with a trembling voice, I expressed my honest thoughts. I explained that while I appreciated the opportunity, I didn't feel I was the right person for the job. I offered to support the project in other ways that aligned with my strengths and capacity.

To my surprise, my boss was not only understanding but also appreciative of my candor. He thanked me for my honesty and for knowing my limits and knowing myself. It was a profound lesson for me. I realized that authenticity, even when it means saying no or admitting limitations, is more valuable than perfection.

When we show up authentically, we create space for others to do the same. We contribute to a culture of honesty and mutual respect. We allow for real connections and meaningful collaborations. And most importantly, we honor our own journey and growth.

From Theory To Transformation: Michael's Story

One of the most powerful transformations I've witnessed as a coach was with my client Michael, a senior marketing executive at a Fortune 500 company. When we first started working together, Michael was the picture of corporate success—impeccably dressed, articulate, and consistently exceeding his targets. But beneath this polished exterior was profound exhaustion and emptiness.

"I feel like I'm playing a character in my own life," he confessed during our sessions. "I've gotten so good at being who I think I need to be that I'm not sure I even know who I really am anymore."

Michael had spent over a decade cultivating a persona he thought was necessary for success. He suppressed his natural creativity and intuition in favor of data-driven decisions that would please his superiors. He hid his quirky sense of humor and passion for environmental causes, fearing they might undermine his authority. He even changed how he dressed and spoke to fit the expected image of an executive at his company.

Our work together began with simple awareness exercises—noticing when he felt most energized versus most drained, identifying situations where he felt he needed to "put on the mask," and reconnecting with values and interests he'd set aside years ago.

The turning point came when Michael decided to bring one authentic element into a high-stakes presentation. Instead of his usual strictly analytical approach, he incorporated a creative storytelling element that felt natural to him. To his surprise, the presentation was his most successful yet, with his CEO specifically commenting on how refreshing and engaging the approach was.

This small success gave Michael the courage to gradually integrate more of his authentic self into his work. He began speaking up in meetings when he disagreed, rather than nodding along. He started mentioning his weekend environmental volunteer work in casual conversations. He even changed his office décor to reflect his personal aesthetic rather than what he thought an executive's office "should" look like.

"The strangest part," Michael told me, "is that being more authentic hasn't hurt my career at all—it's actually accelerated it. People trust me more because they can feel I'm being genuine. And I have so much more energy because I'm not constantly monitoring and adjusting my behavior."

The most profound shift came when Michael's company needed to respond to a major sustainability challenge in their industry. Because he had gradually revealed his passion for environmental issues, he was asked to lead the initiative. The project not only became the most fulfilling work of his career but also positioned him for a promotion that aligned with his authentic interests and values.

"I spent years believing I had to choose between success and authenticity," Michael reflected. "It turns out that authenticity was the missing ingredient in my success all along."

Michael's story illustrates how authenticity isn't just personally fulfilling—it can be professionally advantageous. When we bring our whole selves to our work, we tap into creativity, energy, and connection that simply isn't available when we're wearing a mask.

When you find yourself in a situation that calls for authenticity, your body will often send you signals. For me, if a request makes my chest tighten or a pit form in my stomach, it's a clear sign that I need to pause and check in with myself. The key lies in distinguishing between what feels "light" and what feels "heavy," between what resonates with your truth and what conflicts with it.

Learning to listen to these bodily cues is a practice in itself. It requires slowing down, tuning in, and trusting your inner wisdom. It might feel uncomfortable at first, especially if you're used to overriding your feelings to please others. But with time and practice, it becomes easier to recognize and honor these signals.

The act of authenticity should stem from an overflow of your own self-acceptance and self-love, not from the scanty leftovers after you've depleted yourself in the pursuit of perfection. As I've grown to understand, I'm not here to be perfect. I'm here to be real, to be human, to be me. This realization has been both humbling and empowering. It's allowed me to let go of the exhausting facade of perfection and embrace the beautiful messiness of being human.

Here's what I've discovered: embracing authenticity isn't just for my benefit. When I show up as I am, when I own my strengths and my struggles, it not only allows me to live more fully but also serves as a model for others. It becomes an invitation for people to embrace their own authenticity. As Brené Brown wisely points out, authenticity is a collection of choices that we have to make every day. It's about the choice to show up and be real. The choice to be honest. The choice to let our true selves be seen.

Try This:

- Practice a daily body scan to notice physical reactions to situations and people
- When making decisions, check in with your body's wisdom—does this option feel expansive or constrictive?
- Create a physical gesture (like placing a hand on your heart) to remind yourself to pause and tune into your authentic feelings

Now here's another fun fact about me: I can tell if someone's authentic in 10 minutes or less—it's practically a superpower at this point! When you've interviewed 30,000+ candidates over 18 years, you start picking up on the little clues that separate genuine people from those who are, let's say, creatively curated.

Here's the thing: authenticity shines through in stories, not scripts. I don't need you to have all the right answers (in fact, I prefer it if you don't), but I want to hear real stories with a few bumps and twists. When I ask, "tell me about a time when you faced a challenge," the authentic ones dive right in, no frills. They'll say, "Honestly, I thought I'd messed everything up at first, but here's what I learned…" It's the kind of answer that has humanity baked right into it, not just a polished performance.

Now, if someone's giving me rehearsed answers, it's like they've mentally set up a teleprompter. They might rattle off a response so perfect it belongs in a brochure: "I'm motivated by synergizing strategic paradigms." Synergizing strategic paradigms?! In my head, I'm thinking, "Blink twice if you're real."

Authentic people let themselves show up as they are. They're aware of their strengths and flaws and talk about both with ease. I know someone's authentic when I ask, "what feedback was tough for you to hear?" and they go right there, telling me exactly how it made them feel and what they did to grow. When someone's honest about the messy bits, that's when I know they're the real deal.

If I can get a genuine answer in the first 10 minutes, I know I'm dealing with someone authentic. If not? Well, I'm probably getting an audition for "Best Performance in an Interview," and I'm ready to hand out the award!

FEATURED PRACTICE:
The Authenticity Inventory

Use this exercise to identify areas where you might be living inauthentically and opportunities to bring more of your true self forward:

1. **List your roles**: Write down the various roles you play in your life (e.g., employee, parent, friend, community member).
2. **Rate your authenticity**: For each role, rate from 1-10 how authentic you feel (1 = completely inauthentic, 10 = completely authentic).
3. **Identify masks**: For roles with lower scores, describe the "mask" you wear. What parts of yourself do you hide or exaggerate?
4. **Explore the fear**: For each mask, ask yourself: "What am I afraid would happen if I showed up more authentically in this role?"

5. **Small shifts**: Identify one small way you could bring more authenticity to your lowest-rated role in the coming week.

Research in positive psychology suggests that even small increases in authentic self-expression can create significant improvements in wellbeing.[5] This practice helps you identify specific opportunities for these authentic shifts rather than trying to transform everything at once.

Self-Knowledge: The Foundation of Authenticity

The essence of authenticity lies in knowing oneself deeply and being that rather than trying to be someone else. It's about understanding your own thoughts, emotions, needs, and aspirations. To discover your authentic self, engage in regular self-reflection through journaling or meditation, practice mindfulness to observe your thoughts without judgment, and seek honest feedback from trusted friends. Explore your passions and notice what activities energize you. Challenge your existing beliefs and be open to new experiences that may reveal unknown aspects of yourself. Consider therapy or coaching for professional guidance. Pay attention to your body's reactions in different situations, examine your emotional responses to events, and try crafting a personal mission statement. Remember, self-discovery is an ongoing process that requires patience and compassion. By consistently applying these practices, you'll gradually peel back the layers to reveal your true, authentic self.

It's about being honest with yourself first and foremost. This self-knowledge is the foundation upon which authentic living is built. It requires ongoing self-reflection, curiosity, and a willingness to face uncomfortable truths about ourselves.

For instance, I am highly sensitive and often find myself absorbing others' emotions like a sponge. In the past, I would try to push through this, to be the perfect support for everyone regardless of how it affected me. But now, I make it a point to honor my sensitivity. I set boundaries around my emotional space. I say no more often. I turn down the numerous invitations I get to have coffee with strangers. Old me might have done that. New me takes time to recharge and have more alone time. I live in a house with five boys. Do I need to say more?? I communicate my needs clearer and kinder than I ever have before. And feel zero guilt.

Acknowledging and honoring myself preserves my emotional and spiritual energy, making it easier for me to show up authentically in my relationships and interactions. It allows me to be genuinely present and supportive without losing myself in the process. This self-awareness and self-care have been game-changers in my journey towards authenticity.

Embracing authenticity can be unsettling initially, both for you and for those around you. It requires vulnerability, courage, and a willingness to let go of the illusion of perfection. It means being okay with not always having it all together, with making mistakes, with being a work in progress. This can be particularly challenging in a world that often seems to value polished perfection over raw authenticity. Or, you might upset others who are not ready to face their authenticity.

The key is to be gentle and compassionate with yourself in this process. It's crucial to practice self-acceptance in the moment, to meet yourself where you are with kindness and understanding. A sudden shift to authenticity might initially feel foreign and uncomfortable, but you will soon settle into the profound peace and freedom that comes with being true to yourself. Practice it!

Here are a few examples to get you started: It can be as simple as saying, "I'm having a tough day, and I need some space," or "I'm not sure about this, but I'm willing to try." It's about honoring your truth in each moment, even if it's messy or uncertain. The language you use can be simple and straightforward (and I know, this might be hard at first as you are honoring yourself!).

Psychologists have identified what they call the "authenticity paradox"—while we often fear that showing our true selves will lead to rejection, research consistently shows that authentic self-disclosure actually deepens connection and trust.[6] This paradox appears across personal and professional contexts, challenging our assumption that "putting on a good face" is necessary for acceptance.

In fact, studies show that leaders who acknowledge their limitations and show appropriate vulnerability are rated as more effective and trustworthy than those who maintain a facade of perfection.[7] Similarly, in personal relationships, moments of authentic vulnerability tend to be turning points that deepen intimacy rather than diminish it.

Self-Compassion: The Twin of Authenticity

As we talk about authenticity, it's vital to discuss another cornerstone of personal integrity: self-compassion. Being genuine isn't about being perfectly composed and put together at all times. It's about being kind and understanding with ourselves through the ups and downs of life. Self-compassion is the gentle voice that encourages us to keep going when we stumble, the soothing balm that heals our wounds when we fall.

I struggled to learn this for a long time. I was my own harshest critic, expecting perfection in every aspect of my life. I would berate myself for every mistake, every moment of weakness or uncertainty. It wasn't until I started practicing self-compassion that I was able to truly embrace my authentic self.

I learned to speak to myself as I would to a dear friend—with gentleness, patience, and understanding. I learned to acknowledge my humanity, to accept that I will stumble and fall, and that's okay. I learned to celebrate my efforts and my growth, not just my achievements. This shift in self-talk was transformative. It allowed me to be more honest with myself, to face my shortcomings without fear, and to grow from a place of love rather than criticism.

This shift towards self-compassion has allowed me to show up authentically, without the fear of judgment or the pressure of perfection. It gave me the courage to be seen, to be real, to be me. I found that as I became more compassionate with myself, I naturally became more compassionate with others. My relationships deepened, my work became more fulfilling, and I felt a greater sense of peace and contentment in my daily life.

Research by Dr. Kristin Neff, a pioneer in self-compassion studies, shows that self-compassion is strongly correlated with psychological wellbeing, resilience, and authentic behavior.[8] Contrary to common fears, self-compassion doesn't lead to complacency—it actually motivates greater personal growth and more authentic choices because it removes the barrier of harsh self-judgment that often keeps us stuck in inauthentic patterns.

The 4 A's Framework for Authentic Living

Just as a compass helps you navigate through unfamiliar or challenging terrain, the 4As framework will guide you in your journey towards authenticity and self-compassion.

1. Awareness: Recognize Your Authentic Self and Masks

Be aware of the moments when you're tempted to hide behind a mask. Notice when you're being hard on yourself, when you're expecting flawlessness instead of growth. Awareness is also about recognizing your authentic thoughts, feelings, and needs. This dual awareness—of the perfectionist tendencies and of your true self—lays the foundation for genuine living.

Set aside time each day for self-reflection. Ask yourself, "When did I feel most like myself today? When did I feel the pressure to be someone else?" Write down your observations in a journal. This practice will heighten your awareness and provide valuable insights over time. You might be surprised at the patterns you uncover and the self-knowledge you gain.

Neuroscience research shows that this type of self-reflective awareness activates parts of the brain associated with integrated identity and authentic self-regulation.[9] Regular practice strengthens these neural networks, making authentic responses increasingly natural over time.

Try This:

- Keep an "authenticity journal" where you track moments of both authentic expression and inauthenticity
- Practice a daily meditation focused on observing your thoughts without judgment
- Ask a trusted friend for honest feedback about when you seem most authentic versus when you seem to be wearing a mask

2. Attitude: Embrace Self-Acceptance and Compassion

Embrace an attitude that you are perfectly made just as you are. You are enough, just as you are. Accept who you are with compassion and grace. This doesn't mean you stop growing or improving; it means you approach your growth from a place of self-acceptance rather than self-rejection.

Practice self-compassion by treating yourself as you would a dear friend. When you notice self-critical thoughts, counter them with kind and understanding ones. For example, replace "I'm so stupid for making that mistake" with "I'm human, and humans make mistakes. I'm learning and growing." This shift in attitude can dramatically change how you experience challenges and setbacks.

Studies in positive psychology have found that self-acceptance is a stronger predictor of life satisfaction than factors like wealth, education, or recognition.[10] Developing an accepting attitude toward yourself creates the psychological safety needed for authentic self-expression.

Try This:

- Create a self-compassion mantra that resonates with you and repeat it when self-criticism arises
- Write a letter to yourself from the perspective of a loving friend
- Practice "both-and" thinking: "I both accept myself as I am AND welcome growth and learning"

3. Action: Align Behavior with Your Authentic Self

Take action to align your life with your authentic self. This might mean setting boundaries, expressing your truth, or making choices that honor your values and needs. It's about bringing your inner reality into harmony with your outer expressions and experiences.

Start small. Choose one area of your life where you can practice authenticity today. Perhaps it's expressing a genuine opinion, saying no to a request that doesn't resonate, or sharing a real struggle with a trusted friend. Each authentic action, no matter how small, is a step towards a more genuine life.

Research on psychological congruence (the alignment between inner experience and outer expression) demonstrates that even small authentic actions can reduce anxiety and increase subjective wellbeing.[11] These benefits create a positive feedback loop that reinforces authentic behavior.

Try This:

- Identify one "authenticity stretch" action to take each week
- Practice stating your true feelings or opinions in low-risk situations before building to higher-stakes contexts
- Create a visual reminder (like a bracelet or phone wallpaper) that prompts you to check whether your actions align with your authentic self

4. Alignment: Create Harmony Between Inner Truth and Outer Life

Alignment is the final piece of the puzzle. Ensure that your actions and choices are in alignment with your authentic self. This means living in accordance with your values, passions, and true nature. It's about creating a life that feels true to who you are at your core.

Regularly review your life choices—your relationships, your work, your leisure activities. Put your hand on your heart and ask yourself, "Is this in alignment with my authentic self? Does this resonate with my truth?" And listen closely. Your body tells the truth. It's your body that you must listen to when it comes to understanding alignment. Imagine you're doing a plank—alignment is keeping the frame steady so that you don't collapse.

Longitudinal studies of adult development suggest that people who achieve greater alignment between their values, talents, and daily activities report not only greater subjective wellbeing but also demonstrate greater resilience in the face of life challenges.[12] This alignment creates a sense of coherence that strengthens our sense of self over time.

Try This:

- Conduct a weekly "alignment audit" of how you spent your time and energy
- Gradually restructure parts of your life (career, relationships, activities) to better reflect your authentic self

The Ongoing Journey to Authenticity

Authenticity seems as though it would be simple, but it's an ongoing process, weaving through all the things we need to unlearn from being conditioned by the world. There will be moments of doubt, of fear, of wanting to retreat behind the safety of masks and personas. But each time you choose authenticity, you strengthen your connection to your true self and to the world around you. You create a life that is uniquely, wonderfully yours.

You become the author of your own story. A story that is imperfect, but beautifully, authentically yours. It's a story of growth, of courage, of vulnerability and strength. It's a story that only you can tell.

The journey to authenticity isn't a straight line. It's more like a spiral, where we continually revisit similar themes but with deeper understanding each time. There will be setbacks and moments of doubt. There will be situations where being completely authentic feels too risky or inappropriate. This is all part of the process.

The goal isn't perfect authenticity in every moment—that would be another form of perfectionism. The goal is a growing capacity to recognize, honor, and express your true self with discernment and compassion. It's about progress, not perfection. It's about becoming increasingly comfortable in your own skin, increasingly connected to your own truth, increasingly able to share that truth with the world.

Key Takeaways:

- Authenticity is not just a personal virtue but a foundational element of psychological wellbeing and meaningful connection
- The body provides valuable signals about when we're aligned with or betraying our authentic selves
- Self-compassion is essential for authenticity—we can't be real with others if we're harsh with ourselves

- Contrary to fears, authentic self-expression typically deepens rather than damages connections
- Authenticity is an ongoing journey of unlearning societal conditioning and reconnecting with your true self
- Being authentic doesn't mean being perfect—it means being real, human, and true to yourself

Expert Insights on Authenticity and Self-Compassion

"Authenticity is the daily practice of letting go of who we think we're supposed to be and embracing who we are." — Brené Brown, whose research on vulnerability and authenticity has transformed our understanding of human connection.[13]

"Your task is not to seek for love, but merely to seek and find all the barriers within yourself that you have built against it." — Rumi, whose poetry speaks to the essence of authentic being and self-acceptance.[14]

"Care for your psyche...know thyself, for once we know ourselves, we may learn how to care for ourselves." — Socrates, whose ancient wisdom on self-knowledge remains relevant in our modern search for authenticity.[15]

"To be yourself in a world that is constantly trying to make you something else is the greatest accomplishment." — Ralph Waldo Emerson, whose philosophy celebrated individuality and authentic expression.[16]

Your Turn: Reflective Free Writing

Take a few minutes now to explore your relationship with authenticity. Find a quiet space, set a timer for 10 minutes, and write continuously without editing or judging what comes up. You might consider these prompts:

Free Writing Prompts:

- When do I feel most authentically myself? What people, places, or activities bring out my true nature?
- What parts of myself do I tend to hide or downplay? What fears or beliefs drive this hiding?
- If I were to express one authentic truth that I've been holding back, what would it be? What's stopping me?
- How might my relationships transform if I showed up more authentically in them?

PART III

Creating Your Legacy

Unlocking New Paths

"And when you want something, all the universe
conspires in helping you to achieve it."

— *Paulo Coelho*

What if I told you that you're essentially a complex system of software programs running on the hardware that is your body and brain? Imagine it, algorithms and code dictating your habits, your emotional responses, your thought patterns—essentially everything that makes you, you. Now, what if I told you that you possess the power to rewrite these programs? To reformulate the code of your life, thereby shifting your reality and unlocking new paths to reach your full potential and shine brighter than ever before?

This concept isn't just a fanciful metaphor; it's a powerful way to understand how we can transform our lives. The new program lies within you as you enhance your awareness in understanding and managing your own responses to life's stimuli. It's in the choices you make every day, the thoughts you choose to entertain, the actions you take, and the paths you decide to follow.

Before you write off this concept as abstract nonsense, bear in mind that this isn't a new-age theory. It's as real as the ground beneath your feet. Your paradigms—those fundamental mental programs—are controlling everything from your financial income to your body image to your overall happiness. The only thing standing between you and the life you desire, the only thing preventing you from unlocking your peak potential and shining your brightest light? It's not your circumstances, your past, or even other people. It's you. It's how you think. It's your software program. Remember when we talked about how thoughts turn into things? Master your thoughts, and you master your life.

> **Reflection Moment:** Think about a recurring situation in your life that always seems to produce the same result, despite your best intentions to change it. What automatic "program" might be running in those moments? How might your thoughts be creating this reality?

Mastering your thoughts isn't just about control; it's also about exploration. Think of yourself as the observer of your thoughts. The visual I love for this is that I am literally flying above my body and I'm watching myself like I'm the star character in a movie. Like a scary movie, it's about being willing to venture into uncharted territories of your mind, to question long-held beliefs, to be open to new perspectives and possibilities. It's having the courage to step off the well-trodden path of your current programming and forge a new trail, one that leads to your highest potential and your brightest light.

The Science of Mental Reprogramming

The idea of reprogramming your mind isn't merely metaphorical—it's backed by neuroscience. Research in neuroplasticity has demonstrated that the brain physically changes in response to our thoughts, behaviors, and experiences.[1] With repeated attention and practice, we can actually rewire our neural pathways, strengthening some connections while weakening others.

Studies show that our habitual thoughts and behaviors create neural "superhighways" in the brain—patterns that become increasingly automatic and difficult to change.[2] However, when we deliberately redirect our attention and practice new ways of thinking and responding, we begin to create alternative neural pathways. Over time, with consistent practice, these new pathways can become the dominant ones, effectively changing our default programming.

What's particularly fascinating is that this rewiring happens throughout our entire lives, not just during childhood or adolescence.[3] This means that regardless of your age or how deeply ingrained your current patterns might be, your brain remains capable of remarkable change and adaptation. You literally have the biological capacity to reprogram your mind at any stage of life.

FEATURED PRACTICE:
The Program Interrupt

When you catch yourself in an unwanted mental or emotional program, use this practice to consciously change your programming:

1. **Notice the trigger**: Identify what situation, thought, or sensation activates your unwanted response pattern.
2. **Pause and breathe**: Create a moment of space before your automatic reaction takes over. Take three deep breaths.
3. **Name the program**: Mentally label what's happening: "This is my anger program starting" or "This is my self-doubt routine beginning."
4. **Physical interruption**: Do something unexpected with your body—stand up, change positions, make a silly face, or as I do, break into dance! This physical interruption helps disconnect from the mental pattern.
5. **Choose a new response**: Consciously select a different way to respond—one that aligns with who you want to be.

Neuropsychologist Rick Hanson explains that program interrupts are effective because they momentarily disrupt the brain's automatic processing systems, creating an opportunity to establish new neural connections.[4] The physical component is particularly important as it engages different brain regions, making it harder for the old pattern to reassert itself.

Breaking the Anger Program: My Dance Revolution

So how can you actively rewrite your programming and unlock these new paths? Imagine you're in your early 40s, and you catch yourself in a repetitive cycle. Maybe it's the trigger of your kids yelling at each other that provokes an automatic response of anger within you. That's just the first one that comes to my mind. Ha! Ok, guilty. This one's all me and is the one that I'm still in the process of rewriting. I've got four boys so give me a little credit.

I've been a mom for over a decade and finally now feel like I can control my anger outbursts. So please don't beat yourself up, this takes time and diligence. How do I rewrite my natural tendency to yell/scream/tantrum when provoked? Catching the anger as it's rising in me. Because it's an automatic behavior, it took all my willpower at first to catch the anger rising in the first place. This is where the visual of you rising above your body will help. The first step is intense awareness. Become aware of the automatic behavior. By becoming conscious of the stimulus and your habitual response, you're setting the stage for transformation.

But transformation doesn't stop at awareness. It requires exploration. It demands that you ask yourself, "Is this response serving me? Is it aligned with the person I want to be, the light I want to shine? What other responses could I choose in this moment?"

For some, this understanding may not come easy; it may require unraveling years of conditioning, tracing back to childhood and societal norms. It means filtering out the noise, the external expectations and judgments, to tune into your internal dialogue. How do you actually want to show up in the world? And why can't you?

For me, I realized that the anger goes back several generations. It's what my dad grew up with. And his dad. And his dad. And his dad. For who knows how long. But guess what? You get to be the one that breaks the generational patterns. Through YOU. How cool is that?

Well, a blessing and a curse. I find it exhausting some days. It's like I'm this person who has absolutely no control over myself. Confession: I have yelled at my boys way more than I want to. They have been my greatest teachers in becoming a better human. Here's the strategy I've found: you have to become conscious of the unconscious. In those moments, I tune into the rage I feel coming up inside and then I physically dance it out. Do I look ridiculous? Yes. Does it work? As long as I catch myself before the program takes over and physically do a pattern interrupt. I am now dancing and that somehow takes my brain away from rage into laughter because, well, I crack myself up dancing. My boys are like "what the heck is mom doing" and the rage moment has passed. Victory! Honestly these have become some of my most prized moments of the day, when I can successfully override old programming. BEST DAY EVER. I am becoming a new me!

This isn't a one-size-fits-all solution. I want you to know what worked for me. Your method can be different. Don't judge it, instead explore what gets you out of the program and into the present moment.

The Time I Rewrote My "Too Late" Program

One of my most significant personal reprogramming experiences happened when I was 39 years old. For years, I had been carrying a powerful limiting belief that I had missed my window of opportunity to become a public speaker and author. "If I were going to succeed at that," my mental program insisted, "I would have started in my twenties or early thirties. It's too late now."

This program ran silently in the background, influencing countless decisions without my conscious awareness. I would see speaking opportunities and not apply. I would start writing a chapter for a book and then abandon it, convinced no one would want to read the words of someone who hadn't "made it" by my age.

The pattern interrupt came unexpectedly during a business conference. I was sitting in the audience when a speaker in her sixties took the stage. She radiated confidence and wisdom as she shared her journey—explaining that she had begun her speaking career at 52, after raising her children. The audience was captivated, not despite her age but because of the depth of experience and perspective it gave her.

Something clicked in that moment. I felt a physical sensation—like a lock turning in my chest. I literally whispered to myself, "There goes that excuse."

Back in my hotel room that night, I began the conscious work of rewriting this program. I researched successful authors and speakers who had started later in life. I created a new mantra: "My life experience is my greatest asset, not a liability." Each time the "too late" program tried to run, I would catch it, pause, and consciously choose my new programming instead.

What's fascinating is that once I rewrote this program, I started noticing evidence everywhere that supported my new belief. Stories of late bloomers crossed my path daily. It was as if God had been trying to show me the truth all along, but my old programming had filtered it out.

This experience taught me that many of our most limiting programs operate beneath our conscious awareness, quietly dictating what we believe is possible. But with attention and deliberate effort, even the most persistent mental software can be rewritten, opening doorways to paths we never dared to imagine.

The Mental Fly Swatter: Changing Thought Patterns

Try this on for size: imagine your unwanted habits and/or negative thoughts are pesky flies buzzing around you. Arm yourself with a mental fly swatter and swat those thoughts away as they appear. Each swat is an opportunity to replace a limiting belief with an empowering one, to choose a new path of being.

But don't stop at just replacing negative thoughts with positive ones. Use each swat as an invitation to explore entirely new ways of being, to venture off the binary path of good/bad, positive/negative. Each mental interruption is an opportunity for a mental adventure, a chance to blaze new trails in your mind, an opportunity to choose again.

When we venture off the binary path, we open ourselves to a world of infinite possibilities. Instead of seeing situations as simply good or bad, we can explore the depth of experiences they offer. For instance, a challenging situation at work isn't just "bad"; it could be an opportunity for growth, a chance to develop resilience, or a sign that you're ready for a new direction. Similarly, a "positive" event might carry hidden complexities or lessons. By moving beyond the binary, we can cultivate a more flexible, adaptable mindset that's better equipped to navigate the complexities of life's different paths.

Moreover, venturing off the binary path encourages creativity and innovation. When we're not constrained by rigid categories of right vs. wrong, we're free to make unexpected connections, to see patterns and possibilities that we might otherwise miss. This can lead to novel solutions to problems, fresh approaches to relationships, and innovative ways of living and working.

Make it a conscious practice, and over time, you'll find your inner dialogue undergoes a transformation. But more than that, you'll find your entire mental landscape expands. You'll discover new vistas of thought, new horizons of possibility in these spaces that were once occupied by negativity, shame, blame, and fear.

Try This:

- Practice mental fly-swatting for one specific negative thought pattern this week
- When you "swat" a thought, replace it with three possible alternative perspectives
- Notice how your emotional state shifts when you explore beyond binary thinking

From Theory To Transformation: Emma's Story

One of my coaching clients, Emma, came to me after fifteen years in corporate finance. On paper, she had achieved remarkable success—she had the executive title, the impressive salary, and the respect of her colleagues. But inside, she felt increasingly hollow and disconnected from her work.

"I feel like I'm living someone else's life," she confessed during our first session. "I keep doing what I'm supposed to do, checking all the boxes that should make me successful, but I feel nothing. It's like I'm on autopilot."

Through our coaching work, Emma began to recognize the powerful programming that had shaped her career choices. As the daughter of immigrant parents who had sacrificed everything for her education, she had internalized the belief that success meant financial security above all else. Any interest that didn't lead directly to a lucrative profession was labeled "impractical" or "a hobby" in her mental programming.

What was particularly revealing was Emma's discovery that she had a deep, long-ignored passion for environmental conservation. Since childhood, she had loved nature and felt drawn to work protecting it. But her programming had labeled this path as "financially risky" and "disappointing to her parents."

Our breakthrough moment came when Emma realized she could apply her exceptional financial skills to environmental causes. We explored roles in sustainable investing, finance positions within conservation organizations, and consulting opportunities that would allow her to bridge her expertise with her passion.

The reprogramming wasn't easy. Emma had to consciously catch and redirect thoughts like "This isn't a real career" or "I'm throwing away everything I've built." She practiced pattern interrupts, including physically standing up and changing positions whenever she caught these thoughts arising. She created new mental pathways through research, informational interviews with people in her target field, and regular visualization of her new career direction.

Perhaps the most challenging aspect was reprogramming her definition of what would make her parents proud. Through careful reflection and eventually honest conversations with them, she discovered that their deepest wish was for her happiness and fulfillment, not merely financial success.

Within six months, Emma had secured a position as CFO for an environmental nonprofit—a role that allowed her to leverage her financial expertise while contributing to a cause that deeply resonated with her soul. Her salary decreased, but her sense of purpose and fulfillment skyrocketed.

"I didn't just change careers," Emma told me a year into her new role. "I changed the story I was telling myself about what success looks like. I reprogrammed my definition of a meaningful life. And the amazing thing is, once I gave myself permission to follow this path, all these opportunities appeared that I couldn't see before because my old programming was filtering them out."

Emma's transformation illustrates how deeply our mental programming affects not just our thoughts but our perception of possibilities. When we rewrite our mental software, we literally begin to see options and opportunities that were always there but remained invisible under our old programming.

Redefining Success: Reprogramming Society's Code

The world has "programmed" us to value external markers of success—think GPAs in school, impressive job titles as an adult, and social status. It's easy to lose sight of what true success means to you. But we have the ability to rewrite this mental software, reprogramming our definition of success to align with our authentic self.

This reprogramming isn't about simply swapping one set of values for another. It's about creating a more flexible, adaptive mental framework that allows for continuous growth and exploration. Instead of a rigid code that says, "achieve X to be successful," imagine a program that constantly evolves, adapting to your deepening understanding of yourself and the world.

To begin this reprogramming process, start by questioning the existing code. When you find yourself pursuing a goal, pause and ask: "Is this truly important to me, or is this what I've been programmed to want?" "Is this my mom or dad talking or is this me?" This simple act of questioning begins to create new neural pathways, opening up possibilities you might not have considered before. For example, someone who has been conditioned to be a medical doctor by a family lineage of doctors may decide that the doctor she was raised to be isn't what she wants. Instead, the doctor she truly wants to be is one of psychology, not medical. She then realizes by pursuing this path, she's breaking patterns of the expected and instead, tuning into her natural affinities and gifts to live a more fulfilled life and be on the path that she specifically was called to walk.

FEATURED PRACTICE:
The Success Code Audit

Use this exercise to examine and rewrite your definition of success:

1. **Identify inherited success measures**: List the ways you were taught to measure success (by family, education, society, etc.).
2. **Track your reactions**: For each measure, note your emotional response. Does it energize you or deplete you? Does it feel authentic or imposed?
3. **Trace the origins**: For each measure that feels inauthentic, identify where and when you adopted it. Whose voice is it really?
4. **Draft your success code**: Create your own definition of success based on what truly matters to you—how you want to feel, who you want to be, what legacy you want to leave.
5. **Create visible reminders**: Write your personal success code somewhere you'll see it daily, allowing it to reinforce your new programming.

Research in positive psychology shows that people who define success in terms of personal growth, meaningful relationships, and contribution to others report significantly higher levels of life satisfaction than those who define it primarily through achievement or acquisition.[5]

Rewriting your mental software means you may find that success becomes less about what you achieve and more about how you live. Your beingness. Perhaps your new code prioritizes meaningful connections, personal growth, or leaving a positive impact on the world one smile at a time. The key is to consciously choose the values and beliefs that will form your new programming.

This reprogramming is not a one-time event. Just as software requires regular updates, your mental code needs continuous refinement. Be willing to question your direction, adjust your course, and venture into unknown territories of your psyche. It doesn't matter how old we are when this happens; it's realizing we're constantly conditioned by external factors and it's essential to continually check in with ourselves. Each new experience, each challenge, is an opportunity to update your programming, making it more sophisticated and aligned with your true self.

In this process of mental reprogramming, you'll likely find that your relationship with yourself becomes paramount. After all, you are both the programmer and the computer. Cultivating self-awareness, self-compassion, and self-trust becomes crucial in creating a mental program that serves you well.

The true measure of successful reprogramming isn't how well you conform to societal expectations, but how authentically you express your unique self. As you progressively debug the limiting beliefs of your ego and install new, empowering thought patterns, you'll likely find a sense of peace and fulfillment that's independent of external circumstances.

So, embrace your role as the master programmer of your mind. Start debugging old, limiting beliefs. Install new, empowering thoughts. Run beta tests on new behaviors. It's never too late to initiate a system upgrade. Because ultimately, you are the architect of your mental landscape, the coder of your reality. And what a liberating truth that is to program into your consciousness.

The 4 A's Framework for Mental Reprogramming

In the course of unlocking new paths, the four integral A's— Awareness, Attitude, Action, and Alignment—emerge to guide you:

1. Awareness: Recognize Your Mental Programs

The truth is, you're never going to be able to change anything if you're not aware that there's something to change. Many people go through life on autopilot, reacting to situations rather than acting with intentionality. Do you realize when your emotions are taking the steering wheel? Acknowledging this is the first milestone on the path to rewriting your life code.

But awareness isn't just about recognizing what is; it's also about imagining what could be. It's about being aware of potential, of possibility, of paths not yet taken. When you find yourself in a familiar pattern, a habitual response, take a moment to pause and ask, "What else is possible here? What path have I not yet considered?"

Neuroscience research shows that simply becoming aware of our automatic patterns creates what scientists call "metacognition"—the ability to observe our own thinking processes.[6] This metacognitive awareness activates the prefrontal cortex, the part of the brain responsible for executive function and conscious choice, giving us greater capacity to override automatic programming.

Try This:

- Keep a "pattern journal" for one week, noting recurring thoughts, emotions, or behaviors
- Practice "thought-watching" meditation—simply observing your thoughts without judgment
- Ask trusted friends what patterns they notice in your behavior or responses

2. Attitude: Cultivate Curiosity and Openness

An open attitude isn't just about being positive; it's about being curious. It's about approaching life with a sense of wonder, a willingness to learn and grow. It's about seeing each experience, each person, each moment, as a potential teacher, a potential guide to a new path of understanding and being.

Research in developmental psychology shows that maintaining a curious, exploratory attitude—similar to that of a child—

significantly enhances our ability to learn new patterns and adapt to change.[7] When we approach our mental programming with curiosity rather than judgment, we create the psychological safety needed for deep reprogramming.

Try This:

- When you catch yourself in an old pattern, ask "I wonder what would happen if..." questions
- Approach your thoughts and behaviors with the fascination of a scientist studying an interesting specimen
- Experiment with "beginners mind"—approaching familiar situations as if for the first time

3. Action: Experiment with New Responses

It's about expanding your experience. It's about deliberately choosing to do things differently, to take a different route to work, to start a conversation with a stranger, to say yes to an opportunity that scares you. Each action, each choice, is a step onto a new path, a path that leads to growth, to learning, to new possibilities.

Behavioral psychology confirms that action is essential for rewiring our neural pathways.[8] We can't think our way into new programming—we must act our way there. Each time we respond differently to a familiar trigger, we strengthen new neural connections and weaken old ones, gradually changing our default responses.

Try This:

- Identify one recurring situation and commit to responding differently next time
- Create "if-then" plans: "If [trigger] happens, then I will [new response]"
- Start with small, manageable changes to build confidence for bigger reprogramming efforts

4. Alignment: Integrate New Programming with Your Core Values

The world is a complex web of relationships, and alignment assures that you are in sync with this greater network. It brings not just external success but deep, soulful satisfaction. As you grow and change, as you explore new paths and possibilities, your understanding of your purpose may evolve. Alignment is about staying true to that evolving understanding, about continually reorienting yourself to your highest light.

Research in positive psychology suggests that alignment between our actions and our core values creates a state of "psychological coherence" that is strongly associated with wellbeing and resilience.[9] When our new programming aligns with our deepest values and sense of purpose, it becomes sustainable and life-enhancing.

Try This:

- Regularly check new behaviors against your core values to ensure alignment

- Notice how your body feels when your actions align with your authentic self versus when they don't
- Create a personal mission statement to guide your reprogramming efforts

By focusing on awareness, adjusting your attitude, taking purposeful action, and ensuring alignment, you don't just rewrite your programming; you reclaim it. And in doing so, you aren't merely existing; you are profoundly and joyfully alive.

You are continually evolving. You are continually expanding. You are continually unlocking new potentials, new possibilities, new paths to your brightest light.

Unlocking new paths is about recognizing that you are not a static being, but a dynamic becoming. You are not a fixed point, but an unfolding process. You are not a closed book, but an open-ended story, a story that you are writing and rewriting with every thought, every choice, every action.

Because that's what this journey of life is all about. It's not about reaching a fixed destination; it's about continual exploration. It's about always being willing to take the next step, to learn the next lesson, to embrace the next adventure.

The science of neuroplasticity confirms this view of the self as perpetually evolving. Research shows that our brains continue to create new neural connections throughout our lives, with each experience, each new learning, and each shift in perspective physically changing our brain structure.[10] This means that who you are today is not who you will be tomorrow—not just metaphorically, but biologically.

Embracing this dynamic view of yourself opens up infinite possibilities. Rather than being confined by who you've been or what you've done, you can continuously reinvent yourself, explore new facets of your being, and discover latent potentials that have yet to be expressed.

Key Takeaways:

- Your thoughts, responses, and behaviors are like software programs that can be rewritten
- Program interrupts like physical movement break automatic responses and create space for new choices
- Venturing beyond binary thinking (good/bad) opens up new creative possibilities
- Neuroplasticity means your brain can create new pathways at any age—it's never too late to change
- Your definition of success can be consciously reprogrammed to align with your authentic values
- You are not a fixed entity but a dynamic, evolving process with unlimited potential for growth and transformation

Expert Insights on Mental Reprogramming

"The brain has the ability to reprogram itself without medication, to go from a normal state of working, to better than normal at any age." — Dr. Michael Merzenich, neuroscientist and pioneer in neuroplasticity research.[11]

"Between stimulus and response there is a space. In that space is our power to choose our response. In our response lies our growth and our freedom." — Viktor Frankl, psychiatrist and Holocaust survivor whose work explored human capacity for change even in extreme circumstances.[12]

"Your beliefs become your thoughts, your thoughts become your words, your words become your actions, your actions become your habits, your habits become your values, your values become your destiny." — Mahatma Gandhi, whose life demonstrated the power of conscious reprogramming for personal and social transformation.[13]

"The curious paradox is that when I accept myself just as I am, then I can change." — Carl Rogers, whose client-centered therapy approach recognized that self-acceptance creates the safety needed for deep transformation.[14]

Your Turn: Reflective Free Writing

Take a few minutes now to explore your own mental programming. Find a quiet space, set a timer for 10 minutes, and write continuously without editing or judging what comes up. You might consider these prompts:

Free Writing Prompts:

- What automatic "programs" do you notice running in your life? Which ones serve you, and which limit you?

- What would become possible if you could rewrite one persistent pattern in your life? How might your experience change?
- What inherited definitions of "success" might you be unconsciously following? What would your authentic definition be?
- What pattern interrupts might work for you when you find yourself in automatic reaction mode?

Unlocking Infinite Possibility

"Your life is not a random series of events but a masterpiece in the making, shaped by your beliefs and choices."

-Mike Dooley

Imagine waking up every morning with a sense of purpose, brimming with anticipation. You don't know exactly what will happen, but you're certain of one thing: the potential for life-changing encounters is just one step away. This is an attitude rooted in faith over fear. An attitude that attracts miracles, opportunities, and most importantly, people who can change your life. An attitude that unlocks the infinite potential within you and the boundless possibilities around you. If you are rolling your eyes at me, okay, I see you, but give me a chance here to explain. This CAN become your reality if you choose it. It took me over four decades to finally get it: your life isn't exactly what you want it to be, and you can decide to create something different.

You can *have* what you want, *do* what you want, and most importantly, *be* who you want.

What is one thing you can do today to invite more possibility into your life? Maybe it's reaching out to someone who inspires you, journaling a dream you've been ignoring, or taking five minutes to visualize your ideal future. Begin now! It's okay, put down the book and get busy.

While the concept of infinite possibility might sound mystical, research in psychology and neuroscience offers fascinating insights into how our expectations and beliefs literally shape our reality. Studies in the field of positive psychology have found that people with an "expectation of goodness"—who anticipate positive outcomes and opportunities—actually experience more positive events in their lives.[1]

This isn't just wishful thinking. Neurologically, our brains contain what scientists call a "reticular activating system" (RAS)—a bundle of nerves that filters the millions of bits of information we encounter every day, allowing only a small percentage to reach our conscious awareness.[2] The RAS is heavily influenced by our beliefs and expectations, meaning we literally notice different things depending on what we believe is possible.

When you operate with a mindset of infinite possibility, your RAS becomes programmed to notice opportunities that align with your aspirations—opportunities that may have always been there before but remained invisible under a more limited mindset.

Do you realize the goldmine of possibilities you're sitting on every day? Like we talked about in Chapter 5, those casual chats at a coffee shop, conversations with strangers on a plane, or even simple hellos to your neighbors—any of these interactions can be the moment that turns your life around. But here's the catch: if you aren't deciding and declaring what you're passionate about, speaking what is truly on your heart, and being bold about what you believe, how do you expect others to join you on your journey? The moment you start speaking your truth, you send out an energetic vibration that says, "Hey infinite intelligence, I'm ready. Show me what's next!"

But it's not just about speaking your truth; it's about *believing* in your truth. It's about having an unshakable faith in your potential, in your ability to create the life you desire. For me, that's believing in God. You chose what your belief system is. Whatever it is, when you operate from a space of possibility, you unlock a reservoir of potential within you that you may not even know exists.

Be careful with your words. Your words are only as powerful as the belief behind them. If you speak your dreams but don't truly believe in their possibility, you're sending out a mixed signal. On the other hand, when your words are infused with the unshakable conviction of your potential, you become a magnet for miracles.

FEATURED PRACTICE:
The Possibility Declaration

Use this powerful practice to align your spoken words with your deepest beliefs about what's possible:

1. **Create sacred space**: Find a quiet place where you won't be interrupted. Light a candle or create another small ritual that signifies this is a special time.

2. **Write your declaration**: On a blank page, complete this sentence: "I am ready to create a life where…" Let your imagination soar beyond current limitations.

3. **Speak it aloud**: Stand tall and read your declaration out loud with conviction. Notice any internal resistance or doubt that arises.

4. **Refine for alignment**: Rewrite any parts where you felt dishonesty or disbelief until your whole body resonates with the truth of your words. This make take several attempts. Keep the faith.

5. **Share it strategically**: Identify three people who will support your vision, and share your declaration with them (this one is totally optional)

Research by Dr. Nathaniel Branden, pioneer in the psychology of self-esteem, shows that verbally declaring our intentions while in a state of emotional alignment significantly increases our commitment and follow-through.[3] By speaking our possibilities aloud to supportive others, we create a powerful accountability mechanism that neurologically reinforces our commitment.

From Thought to Television:
My Twin Cities Live Story

One of my most profound experiences with infinite possibility happened in spring 2024. I was taking my morning walk, enjoying the fresh air and letting my mind wander to new possibilities. Out of nowhere, a clear thought formed in my mind: "I'd love to be on local television to share my message about purpose and authenticity." I didn't analyze it too much—I simply acknowledged the desire and continued my walk, letting the thought settle into my consciousness.

Just three days later—yes, only three days!—a mutual friend introduced me to a woman named Sarah. We had a wonderful conversation about personal development and the importance of living authentically. As we were wrapping up our chat, she looked at me thoughtfully and said, "You know, I could totally see you appearing on television. You have such a natural way of explaining complex concepts about purpose."

I smiled and glanced upward, immediately recognizing this synchronicity for what it was. God was all over this. Infinite intelligence was responding to a thought I'd had just days before.

"That's funny you should mention that," I said. "I was just thinking about exploring television opportunities."

Then came the stunning revelation. "My best friend is actually one of the producers of Twin Cities Live," Sarah continued. "I'm having dinner with him next week. Would you like me to mention you?"

Of course, I said yes. I shared with her my vision for helping people reconnect with their purpose and authentic selves. She took notes on her phone, nodding enthusiastically, and promised to pass along my information.

True to her word, Sarah made the connection. Within a month, we had confirmed a date for my first television appearance.

As the day approached, I prepared diligently. I walked around outside my house, rehearsing my talking points at least 50 times. I wanted to make sure I could convey my message about pursuing your purpose clearly and concisely, even with the pressures of being on camera. There were moments of nervousness, of course—this was a completely new experience for me—but the nervousness was overshadowed by an electric sense of alignment. This opportunity felt meant to be.

Six weeks after that initial thought during my morning walk, I was in the studio, getting ready for my first appearance on Twin Cities Live. Sitting under the bright lights, sharing my passion for helping people pursue their purpose, was one of the most exhilarating moments of my life. And I know there are so many more to come.

This experience taught me that when you put a desire out into the universe with clear intention, stay open to unexpected connections, and then take aligned action when opportunities present themselves, magical things can happen. What's remarkable isn't just that I manifested a television appearance—it's the effortless way it unfolded, through a series of "coincidences" that were anything but random.

The universe, God, divine intelligence truly does conspire to help us—but first, we must be brave enough to acknowledge our desires, remain open to unexpected pathways, and say "yes" when possibility knocks on our door. The possibilities are always there; our job is to expand our awareness to recognize them and our courage to act on them when they appear.

The Contagious Energy of Possibility

When you're attuned to the "anything is possible" frequency, you draw in the unexpected. You begin to shift from an "I hate Mondays, nothing good is going to happen today" mindset to one teeming with aliveness, possibility, wonder, and curiosity. This energy isn't something you keep to yourself; it's contagious. People want to be around someone who believes that miracles happen every day and they can happen to you.

But more than that, people want to be around someone who believes in their own miracles. When you have faith in your own potential, when you operate from a space of knowing that you are capable of creating the life you desire, you inspire others to do the same. You become a living, breathing example of the power of unlocking one's peak potential.

Here's a scenario some of you may find familiar: you're the go-to person for uplifting and cheering on everyone else in your circle. You give your knowledge and expertise, and you give generously. But pause for a moment and ask yourself, "Who's there to lift me up?" If you find that you're consistently the most driven individual in your environment, then it's time to find a new "room," metaphorically speaking.

When you're immersed in an environment of lack—where people are more likely to pull you down than cheer you on—

you will innately begin to operate differently to fit into that tribal culture. On the flip side, when you align with dreamers, visionaries, and entrepreneurs who are bold, courageous, and just as excited about making the world a better place as you are, you open doors to unlimited potential.

Research in social psychology confirms this environmental effect through what scientists call "social contagion"—the tendency for emotions, beliefs, and behaviors to spread through social networks almost like a virus.[4] Studies show that we are dramatically influenced by the five people we spend the most time with, unconsciously adopting their expectations, energy levels, and beliefs about what's possible.

But it's not just about finding the right tribe; it's about being the right tribe. It's about embodying the qualities you wish to attract. If you want to be surrounded by people who believe in their potential, start by believing in yours. If you want to be part of a culture of abundance, start by cultivating an abundant mindset. The external always reflects the internal.

Think about the people you surround yourself with. Are they fueling your dreams or dousing them? The impact of your circle is tremendous. So, if the conversations you're having don't align with your aspirations, it's time for some proactive changes.

And if you're looking around, realizing this is true, but you don't see what you're looking for, then create it. Envision the circle you want—imagine how it feels to be part of it, the types of conversations you'll have, and the emotional atmosphere. What kind of information are these dreamers and visionaries sharing? What collective emotions are flooding the room? Hold that image.

Visualize it. Believe it's on the way. If the kind of circle of people you want to surround yourself with doesn't exist—create it first by your intentional thought that it's possible.

A few years ago I yearned for a circle of female friends who were not just in the business world, but also believers like me. I closed my eyes and visualized the kinds of friendship I wanted to have. Friends who sent you cards in the mail just because. Friends who showed up to the significant events not because you asked them but because they know what's important to you. Friends who call when you're having a down week. And guess what? Less than a year later I had a circle of women who embody this. I saw it in my mind first and envisioned it like it existed. Soon it became real. These women are such a light in my life, and I am so thankful that I held strongly to a faith that they were on their way.

Try This:

- Identify one environment in your life that limits your sense of possibility
- Take one action this week to either transform that environment or reduce your time in it
- Commit to spending more time with at least one person who expands your sense of what's possible for you

It's important to point out that the greatest limitation you will ever face is not the circumstances around you, but the doubts within you. You know that voice that tells you that it's too hard, that you'll never reach your goals, that you're not good enough?

The doubter of your infinite possibilities must shift. The moment you shift from "I can't" to "I can," from "I'm not" to "I am," you unleash a force within you that is unstoppable.

Like Henry Ford said, "Whether you think you can or you think you can't, you're right."

I fully listened to my doubter more than I care to admit. I told myself the narrative that life was hard, and it would be easier to give up on several big goals I was working towards. One of those goals was to give my first big keynote speech. The story I told myself was that my voice didn't matter, no one would show up, and I would freeze on stage anyway. Wow—seriously Laura. Harsh. It wasn't until I hired a coach to push me. She forced me to put a date on the calendar and begin to write the keynote. Over 100 people showed up in January 2024 for it. I worked incredibly hard on the speech, practiced it at least 50 times like I shared with you in chapter eight and wow, it was one of the most exhilarating moments of my life to stand up in front of that crowd. I crushed it! I believed in myself, I put in the work, and I moved the audience. I am certain there will be more of those moments in the future.

I had to release the limits, release the fears, and allow spirit to move in me. When I leaned back, relaxed, and allowed a greater power to guide me—magic happened.

From Theory to Transformation: Jennifer's Story

A coaching client whose journey exemplifies the power of unlocking infinite possibility is Jennifer, a

52-year-old healthcare administrator who came to me convinced that certain dreams were simply "too late" for her.

Jennifer had spent 27 years at the same company, gradually climbing the administrative ladder. On paper, she was successful—she had the impressive title, the comfortable salary, the respect of her colleagues. But in our first coaching session, she confessed that she had abandoned her deepest aspiration decades ago.

"I always wanted to be an innovator," she told me, her voice barely above a whisper, as if even speaking the dream aloud might invite ridicule. "I have ideas for patient care solutions that could really make a difference. But at my age, with no entrepreneurial experience...it's just not realistic."

Jennifer's limiting beliefs were palpable: "I'm too old to start something new." "I don't have the right connections." "No one will take me seriously." "I can't risk financial stability at this point in my life."

Our first task was to challenge these beliefs. I asked Jennifer to identify the source of each limitation and to question whether it was an absolute truth or simply a fear masquerading as fact. As she explored this question, she realized most of her "can'ts" were actually "won't allow myself to."

Then we shifted to possibility thinking. Instead of focusing on all the reasons her dream couldn't happen, we explored what it might look like if it could. What first steps would be possible without disrupting her current stability? Who in her existing network might support this vision? What small action could she take that would feel exciting rather than terrifying?

Jennifer decided to start a simple blog sharing her ideas for healthcare innovation. This relatively low-risk step required no one's permission but her own. To her surprise, her posts began generating interest and comments from other healthcare professionals. One post caught the attention of a former colleague who worked at a healthcare technology startup.

This connection led to an invitation to speak at a small healthcare innovation conference. With some coaching and practice, Jennifer delivered a compelling talk about her patient care concepts. The response was enthusiastic, and several attendees approached her afterward wanting to discuss her ideas further.

Within eight months of our first meeting, Jennifer had been offered a part-time consulting role with the startup while maintaining her administrative position. This arrangement allowed her to test the waters of innovation without sacrificing her financial security. A year later, she had transitioned to full-time innovation work, co-developing a patient care application that was being piloted in three hospitals.

What strikes me most about Jennifer's transformation wasn't just the external changes—impressive as they were—but the internal shift in her relationship with possibility. During a recent coaching session, she reflected on this evolution:

"I realize now that what I thought was impossible wasn't actually impossible at all," she said. "It was just unfamiliar. And unfamiliar feels scary until you take that first step. Then another. And another. Now I look at my life and wonder what else might be possible that I've been ruling out."

Jennifer's story illustrates how the future is created twice: first in our imagination and then in reality. By expanding her sense of what was possible, by surrounding herself with supporters rather than doubters, and by taking consistent action from a place of faith rather than fear, she transformed not just her career but her entire relationship with possibility itself.

Her journey reminds us that our infinite potential doesn't have an expiration date. At any age, in any circumstance, we can choose to see beyond our current limitations and step into the vast field of possibility that has been waiting for us all along.

Now I'm not saying that life is perfect sunshine and rainbows. Not at all.

Even with the best intentions, life can throw curveballs that might knock you off your path. That's okay. Your journey isn't a straight line; it's a spiral. You'll come back to the same challenges, but you'll approach them with higher levels of consciousness. Use these moments as checkpoints to reflect, reset, and realign. Are you still in tune with yourself? If not, what needs to change?

You are not defined by your circumstances; you are defined by your response to those circumstances. Every challenge is an opportunity to grow, to evolve, to unlock a new level of your peak potential. When you approach life with this mindset, there are no dead ends, only new beginnings.

Research in resilience psychology shows that what separates highly resilient people from others isn't an absence of challenges but rather their interpretation of those challenges.[5] While many see obstacles as proof of their limitations, resilient individuals view them as opportunities to develop new capabilities. This "challenge mindset" actually activates different neurological pathways than a "threat mindset," enabling more creative problem-solving and greater access to our inner resources.[6]

FEATURED PRACTICE:
The Possibility Reframe

When facing a challenge or setback, use this practice to shift from limitation to possibility:

1. **Acknowledge reality**: Start by honestly naming the challenge without minimizing or catastrophizing.
2. **Identify the limitation story**: Write down the limiting interpretation your mind is creating (e.g., "This proves I'm not meant to succeed").
3. **Find the growth opportunity**: Ask: "How might this challenge be preparing me for something greater?" and "What capabilities might I develop by facing this?"
4. **Generate possibility questions**: Replace "Why is this happening to me?" with "What might be possible because of this?" and "How might this redirect me toward something even better?"

5. **Take aligned action**: Identify one small step that comes from your new possibility perspective rather than your limitation story.

Studies show that this type of cognitive reframing significantly impacts our stress response, reducing cortisol levels and activating the brain's executive functions rather than its threat-response systems.[7] This doesn't mean denying reality or forcing toxic positivity—it means finding genuine possibility within reality.

Yes, life on Earth is complex. We can't dismiss our human experiences or the tangible reality we operate within. But there's more than just A+B=C. There's room for divine intervention, for the magical and the mystical, for "God moments" that defy logic. It's not either-or; it's both-and. It's integrating the practical with the spiritual, marrying human action with divine guidance.

And when you operate from this space of divine connection, you tap into a potential that is truly limitless. You begin to understand that you are not just a physical being having a spiritual experience, but a spiritual being having a physical experience. You begin to see that your potential is not bound by the limitations of the material world, but is infinitely expansive, just like the spirit that animates you.

The 4 A's Framework for Unlocking Infinite Possibility

1. Awareness: Recognize the Unlimited Potential Within and Around You

The "turning points" and "unscheduled magic" in your life aren't just luck or fate; they are manifestations of your inner state. Scan your life with a metaphorical magnifying glass. Do you have destructive thoughts that aren't serving your purpose? Your financial well-being, physical health, and even the quality of your relationships are all direct reflections of your inner state. Acknowledge this, and you'll find it easier to spot opportunities and seize them. When you operate from this space of awareness, you begin to see that the limitations you perceive are not real, but merely illusions created by your own mind.

Research in cognitive psychology reveals that our perception is highly selective—we literally see what we expect to see.[8] When we become aware of our limiting expectations, we can consciously expand our perceptual filters to notice possibilities that were always present but previously invisible to us.

Try This:

- Keep a "possibility journal" where you record unexpected opportunities each day
- Practice "expectation awareness" by noticing when you automatically assume limitation

- Ask three trusted friends what possibilities they see for you that you might be overlooking

2. Attitude: Choose Faith Over Fear

Here's where your faith overtakes fear. Your beliefs act as a filter through which you see the world. Imagine if you viewed each encounter as an opportunity waiting to be seized. Would your conversations sound the same? Absolutely not! You'd seek depth, ask questions that invoke thought, and lean into discussions that challenge your perspectives. That's the attitude of someone who doesn't just wait for miracles but actively co-creates them as you partner with God. It's about having the audacity to dream big and the tenacity to make those dreams a reality. When you adopt this attitude, you unlock a level of potential that most people never dare to access.

Studies in neuroscience have identified what researchers call the "expectation effect," where our expectations literally shape our perceptions and experiences.[9] When we adopt an attitude of possibility rather than limitation, different neural networks activate, allowing us to see opportunities and solutions that remain invisible under a fear-based mindset.

Try This:

- Start each day by declaring three things you believe are possible for you

- When fear arises, acknowledge it but consciously choose faith instead
- Surround yourself with physical reminders of previous "impossible" things that became reality

3. Action: Create Your Reality

How do you turn that wonderful vision into your everyday reality? You take action, no matter how small. Volunteer at organizations that align with your passions, publish articles that reflect your viewpoints, initiate projects that embody your dreams. It doesn't have to be monumental—start small, but start. Each tiny step brings you closer to a more focused vision of your life. If you want to create a life of joy, start by being the joy you wish to experience. You get to choose.

Research in behavioral psychology demonstrates that action creates a positive feedback loop with our beliefs and perceptions.[10] When we take action based on possibility rather than limitation, we create evidence that reinforces our belief in what's possible, which in turn inspires more expansive action.

Try This:

- Identify one "possibility action" you can take today, no matter how small
- Create accountability by sharing your action commitments with a possibility-minded friend
- Celebrate evidence of possibility that shows up in response to your actions

4. Alignment: Harmonize Mind, Body, and Soul

When your actions resonate with your innermost desires, you'll notice an incredible thing happening. Those "coincidental" meetings or "lucky" opportunities will multiply because you've set the stage for synchronicities to occur. At this stage, you're not just manifesting; you're co-creating your reality. It's about honoring your unique path, even if it looks different from everyone else's. When you live in alignment with your truth, you unlock a flow of potential that is truly unstoppable.

Alignment isn't just spiritual; it encompasses every facet of your existence. Just as you nourish your mind with knowledge and your body with healthy habits, your soul too needs its form of sustenance. It could be through meditation, prayer, or even silent moments of gratitude. Balancing these pillars—mind, body, soul—will not just align you with your goals but also bring an unparalleled sense of peace and satisfaction.

But more than that, it will bring you a sense of wholeness. When you are aligned in mind, body, and soul, you are no longer fragmented. You are no longer at war with yourself. You become a unified force, a being of pure potential, ready to manifest your deepest desires and create a life beyond your wildest dreams.

Research in the field of psychoneuroimmunology shows that when our thoughts, emotions, behaviors, and values are in alignment, our physiological systems function optimally.[11] This state of coherence enhances our health, creativity, and ability to recognize and act on opportunities.

Try This:

- Conduct a daily alignment check-in with all aspects of yourself: mind, body, emotions, spirit
- Notice when you feel most "in flow" and identify the alignment factors present in those moments
- Create regular practices that nourish all dimensions of your being

You're standing at the precipice of incredible life changes, and all you need to do to tip the scales in your favor is to speak up, expect the magical, and surround yourself with those who elevate you.

Most importantly, you must believe in yourself. You must have an unshakable faith in your ability to create the life you desire internally first before it shows up on the external. God didn't place dreams in your heart that are supposed to die. They are meant to come into your reality.

The journey to unlocking infinite possibility is both deeply personal and universally available. It's not reserved for a special few—it's your birthright as a human being. The only question is whether you're ready to claim it.

As you move forward, I invite you to live from a place of possibility rather than limitation. To see obstacles as opportunities, strangers as potential allies, and challenges as growth catalysts. To speak your truth boldly, believing that the universe/God/infinite intelligence is conspiring to help you achieve your deepest desires.

Because it is. I know this in my bones, have lived it in my experience, and have witnessed it countless times in the lives of my clients. Infinite possibility isn't just a nice idea—it's the fundamental truth of our existence. And once you recognize this truth, your life will never be the same.

Key Takeaways:

- Your potential is not limited by external circumstances but by your beliefs about what's possible
- The people you surround yourself with dramatically influence your sense of possibility
- Both practical action and faith are essential elements of manifesting possibilities
- Your beliefs literally shape what you perceive as possible in your world
- Life's challenges are opportunities to approach familiar limitations with new levels of consciousness
- Inner alignment creates outer synchronicity, bringing unexpected opportunities into your path

Expert Insights on Infinite Possibility

"When you change the way you look at things, the things you look at change." — Wayne Dyer, whose research and teaching on intention and manifestation has transformed millions of lives.[12]

"The universe will rearrange itself to accommodate your picture of reality. If you believe in limitation, limitation will surround you. If you believe in possibility, possibility surrounds you." — Deepak Chopra, whose integration of quantum physics and consciousness explores how reality conforms to our expectations.[13]

"Faith is taking the first step even when you don't see the whole staircase." — Martin Luther King Jr., whose life demonstrated the power of acting from possibility rather than being constrained by present limitations.[14]

"The future belongs to those who believe in the beauty of their dreams." — Eleanor Roosevelt, whose work embodied the transformation possible when we act from vision rather than limitation.[15]

Your Turn: Reflective Free Writing

Take a few minutes now to explore your relationship with possibility. Find a quiet space, set a timer for 10 minutes, and write continuously without editing or judging what comes up. You might consider these prompts:

Free Writing Prompts:

- What becomes possible in my life if I truly believe that infinite potential is available to me?
- Where in my life am I operating from limitation rather than possibility? What would change if I shifted this perspective?
- Who are the people in my life who expand my sense of what's possible? How can I spend more time with them?
- What dream or aspiration have I been hesitant to speak aloud? What's the first step toward making it real?
- If I knew the universe was conspiring to help me succeed, what would I pursue that I've been afraid to attempt?

Unlocking Your Impact

"The meaning of life is to find your gift. The purpose of life is to give it away."

– Pablo Picasso

Have you ever pondered the ripple effect of your existence? If not, let me invite you to sit with this for a moment before moving on. Because it's important to recognize how significant your presence in this world truly is.

So pause, shut off the noise, and just think about the ripple effects of every positive word, action, or step—whether tiny or significant—that you've made in your time here in this world.

Pause.

Pause.

Pause.

> **Reflection Moment:** Take a moment to recall three instances where your actions, however small, positively affected someone else's life. How did it make you feel? How might that person have been changed by your impact?

The truth is, your impact is far greater than you can possibly imagine. Every interaction you have, every choice you make, every thought you think, sends out a ripple that touches countless lives, often in ways you may never know.

You never know whom you're impacting just by being yourself. A smile, a kind word, or even a simple act of integrity—these are potent catalysts for change. But what happens when we cloak ourselves in personas that don't align with who we truly are?

We all wear masks, consciously or not, created by the world's perceptions of success and love. These false identities tell us how to operate in the world. They dictate how we fill our limited time with our ambitions, careers, hobbies, and day-to-day activities.

For most of us, we know it doesn't feel right. But it can be uncomfortable to separate ourselves from the majority, especially when there doesn't seem to be anything wrong with where we're headed.

Our brains may say otherwise, but we are not just the sum of our roles or occupations. We must break free from defining ourselves by our job titles and assuming that our credentials dictate where we can go. The people you are meant to work with and do live with will appreciate your authentic self, even if it doesn't fit neatly into societal norms and expectations.

From Theory to Transformation: Carl's Story

I distinctly remember when I was 29 and working as an executive recruiter, a 52 year old man—that we'll call him Carl—came into my office. My job was to interview him to see if he was a good fit for a role I was looking to fill.

During our conversation, I asked him why he was looking for a new job and Carl proceeded to tell me his life story. I'll have to summarize it here, but he told me that he thought the best way to support his family was by providing them with as much money as possible and a comfortable life. To that end, Carl took every promotion as they came up, traveled overseas often and worked and worked and worked. He ended up missing most of his kids' activities and ended up gettin a divorce.

Carl was in my office because the company that had employed him for 25 years had let him go. He was clearly still in shock and processing out loud with me. He flat out told me he regretted that he lived inauthentically. Carl put on a mask for so many years being the man he was told by society and his parents "was right" that he lost sight of who he really was. Now at age 52, I could tell he felt compelled to figure out who he really was and toss old paradigms out the window.

There was a long pause, and I knew exactly what he was thinking because I was thinking it as well: he needed to let go of everyone else's expectations of who he's supposed to be and go out and find himself. I looked at Carl and said, "You better get the heck out of my office. Forget about returning to a corporate job, Carl. Go explore." We shook hands, then hugged. Today Carl has a coaching business and runs men's groups in Florida. He is thriving.

So the question for us all is, why wait for a wake-up call like Carl?

Here's the first step to beginning to unlock your impact: love yourself.

Ok, ok, before I lose you completely, hang with me here.

Inspired by Louise Hay's "You Can Heal Your Life," I started doing the exercises she suggests in her book. Have you ever stood in front of a mirror, looked at yourself intently in that mirror and said the words "I love you"? Wow, is this powerful.

At first, I said it but I didn't feel any substance behind it. Kind of like those encounters where someone asks you "how are you" in passing, but they don't really want you to share an answer other than "good" or "fine." I said the words. But there wasn't real truth or emotion to the words.

In short, I had work to do.

If you've been at a point where you couldn't look in the mirror and say, "I love you," know that you're not alone. This is a common struggle, but one worth overcoming. Standing in front of the mirror, telling yourself, "I love you" can be transformative.

It's as if you're seeing your reflection—your real self— for the first time.

FEATURED PRACTICE: THE MIRROR EXERCISE

Purpose: To develop self-love and authenticity through direct affirmation

Steps:

1. Stand in front of a mirror where you can see your face clearly
2. Look directly into your own eyes

3. Say aloud: "I love you" with intention and focus
4. Notice any resistance or discomfort that arises
5. Continue the practice daily, allowing the words to become more genuine over time
6. Eventually, add specific affirmations: "I love you and I accept you exactly as you are"

Expert Insight: *"The mirror exercise is one of the most powerful tools for healing our relationship with ourselves. When we can look at ourselves with love and acceptance, we begin to transform how we show up in the world."* — Dr. Kristin Neff, self-compassion researcher and author of "Self-Compassion: The Proven Power of Being Kind to Yourself"

And as you see your real self, you also see the potential for your real impact. You see how loving yourself fully and authentically allows you to love others more deeply. You see how embracing your truth empowers others to do the same.

Many of the world's issues arise from a lack of self-love. Egos drive wars, fuel greed, and sow discord. Imagine if we all loved ourselves, how we could dramatically shift our world towards compassion, love, and understanding.

Imagine the ripples that would create. Imagine the tsunamis of change that would wash over the world. This is the great healing that occurs when love rules.

Awareness: Seeing Your Impact

> "The first step toward change is awareness. The second step is acceptance." — Nathaniel Branden

Let's explore the first A in our framework: Awareness. Start by becoming aware of the masks you wear and the personas you adopt. These often serve as coping mechanisms that could be shielding your true self. Deepen your understanding of your core desires, fears, and strengths. This heightened self-awareness is the first step in removing the layers that obscure your authenticity. Start noticing how your energy affects those around you. Pay attention to the subtle shifts in a room when you enter it. Become conscious of the power of your presence.

For example, if someone cuts you off in traffic, the new you, the one in the process of loving yourself and loving others, may feel an innate understanding. Instead of reacting with anger, you respond with compassion. Maybe this person was on their way to the hospital. Maybe they just lost someone they love. Now of course you have no idea why they cut you off in traffic, but isn't it more joyful to live with compassion than animosity?

This reaction reveals a more accepting nature—the rebirth of the old self into the new. The real indicator of progress lies in the ability to bounce back if you do slip in certain moments, to not wallow in self-pity, but to seize the steering wheel and get back on track.

AWARENESS EXERCISE

Try this exercise: For one week, at the end of each day, reflect on your interactions. How did you impact others? How did others impact you? What ripples did you create, intentionally or unintentionally? This practice will heighten your awareness of your influence and help you become more intentional about the impact you want to have.

> **Reflection Moment:** What is one interaction today where you noticed your impact on someone else? How might you have approached it differently with greater awareness?

Attitude: Believing in Your Power

Shifting your attitude from fear to faith, from skepticism to optimism, allows you to embrace your authentic self who is ripe for impact. This mental reorientation clears the path for positive actions, enriches your experiences, and opens up possibilities for true joy and fulfillment. Do you believe that you have the power to change lives, to shift energies, to make a difference? Your belief in your own impact, or lack thereof, will shape the ripples you send out.

Consider adopting a "ripple mindset." With every interaction, every decision, remind yourself: "This matters. This has an impact." Even small actions can create powerful ripples. Believe in the significance of your presence and actions, and you'll naturally become more intentional about the impact you create.

And each time you choose compassion over anger, understanding over judgment, you send out a ripple. You contribute to a shift in the collective energy. You make an impact, however small it may seem in the moment.

Dr. Carol Dweck, Stanford psychologist and author of "Mindset: The New Psychology of Success," found in her research that people with a "growth mindset"—those who believe their abilities can be developed through dedication and hard work—are more likely to achieve success than those with a "fixed mindset." Similarly, when we adopt an "impact mindset"—believing that our actions create meaningful ripples—we become more intentional about our interactions and more aware of our influence.

Action: Creating Ripples of Change

Whether you're setting boundaries, pursuing your passions, or making lifestyle changes, your actions will resonate on a higher frequency when they reflect your true self. This, in turn, broadens the scope of your impact and serves as a catalyst for change in both your life and the lives of others.

By the way, your actions don't have to be grand gestures. In fact, it's often the small, daily actions that have the most profound impact. It's the way you choose to respond to a frustrating situation. It's the moment you take to really listen to someone. It's smiling and conversing with the grocery store clerk. It's the courage to speak your truth, even when your voice shakes. These are the actions that send out the most powerful ripples.

Challenge yourself to take one intentional, positive action each day. It could be as simple as sending an encouraging message to a friend, picking up litter in your neighborhood, or volunteering for a cause you care about. Remember, every action, no matter how small, has the potential to create significant ripples.

FEATURED PRACTICE: DAILY INTENTIONAL IMPACT

Purpose: To create conscious positive ripples through deliberate action

Steps:

1. Each morning, set an intention for one positive impact you want to make that day
2. Make it specific and achievable (e.g., "I will genuinely compliment someone today")
3. Throughout the day, look for opportunities to fulfill your intention
4. Take the action with full awareness and presence
5. In the evening, reflect on the experience and any observable effects
6. Journal about how it felt to create this intentional impact

I get asked all the time, how do I find my purpose? There are many paths to purpose, but one of the prompting questions that gets you to think deeply about their purpose is to reflect on your pain. Your pain? Yes, your pain. What have you gone through and come out the other side a changed person?

I have countless stories on purpose from taking hundreds of people through my purpose workshop, but one that stands out is my friend Jill. Jill went through a very painful divorce. There's an exercise we do in the workshop that helps participants understand the people they most desire to serve. Jill did this exercise and she was so excited to share with the rest of the class that she wants to serve others who are navigating divorces like she did. Today, Jill serves others who are going through divorces, helping them navigate the emotional and practical challenges she once faced. Her pain became her purpose, her struggle became her strength, and now she's making a profound impact on others going through similar experiences.

And in this way, our impact becomes immeasurable. We become walking, talking, living, breathing invitations for others to step into their truth, to love themselves fully, to send out their own ripples of change.

Alignment: Finding Harmony

Finding harmony is a key in alignment. For those who view life through a spiritual lens, this could mean being in harmony with the ultimate Creator. Alignment brings about serendipities and what some might call "God moments," where everything seems to fall into place effortlessly, reinforcing your path of authenticity.

Alignment isn't just about feeling good. It's about recognizing that when you're in alignment, your impact is amplified. When you're living in your truth, when you're shining your unique light, you become a beacon for others. You attract those who need your specific energy, your particular brand of magic.

To cultivate alignment, regularly check in with yourself. Ask: "Am I living in a way that aligns with my values? Am I using my unique gifts to serve others? Am I creating the kind of impact I want to have in the world?" If the answer is no, begin today by making a promise to yourself to pick one area of your life that feels off and ask for guidance from within to begin restoring harmony.

Key Takeaways:

- Your impact matters: Every interaction, every choice, every thought creates ripples that touch countless lives.
- Self-love is foundational to creating positive impact in the world
- Small, daily actions often create the most powerful ripples of change
- Authenticity amplifies impact — when you're truly yourself, your presence becomes a catalyst for positive change in others
- As you take this journey, as you step more and more into your truth, your impact will grow. The ripples you send out will become waves, touching shores you may never see, changing lives you may never know.
- Who you are is a powerful force for change in this world. Your authenticity, your self-love, your courage to be real—these are the seeds of your impact. As you nurture these qualities in yourself, you create a fertile ground for others to do the

same. Don't underestimate the power of your presence, your words, and your actions.

Expert Insights

"Owning our story and loving ourselves through that process is the bravest thing we'll ever do." — Brené Brown, research professor at the University of Houston, who has spent two decades studying courage, vulnerability, shame, and empathy. Her research reveals that people who have a strong sense of worthiness share one thing in common: they believe they are worthy of love and belonging.[1]

"The universe is not outside of you. Look inside yourself; everything that you want, you already are." — Rumi, whose poetry and spiritual teachings continue to influence our understanding of inner light and authentic connection.[2]

"When you make a choice, you change the future." — Deepak Chopra, whose research and teachings on consciousness demonstrate how our choices create ripple effects throughout our lives and the world.[3]

Your Turn: Reflective Free Writing

Alright, you know the drill by now. Grab your journal or use the space below to anchor in your learnings from this chapter. Here are your prompts:

1. Think about the positive ripples you've created in others' lives. Start with: "I may not have realized it at the time, but I created ripples when I…"

2. Imagine and describe the impact you could have if you were living completely authentically. What would change? Who would be affected? What ripples would you create? Start with: "If I were living fully as my authentic self, my impact would…"

CHAPTER

Unlocking Your Pen

"You are not a fallen victim of circumstance but a rising hero co-authoring your life with divine intelligence, actively shaping your story with each conscious choice, reframing challenge as opportunity, and transforming not just your own life but creating a legacy of possibility for others."

–Brendon Burchard

Throughout this chapter, we'll explore how to become the conscious co-author of your life using the 4 A's Framework—Awareness, Attitude, Action, and Alignment. While previous chapters focused on reconnecting with your worth, truth, joy, gifts, confidence, trust, purposeful action, authenticity, mental reprogramming, infinite possibility, and meaningful impact, this final chapter centers on perhaps the most empowering truth of all: you have the pen. You are not merely a character in a predetermined script but a creative partner with divine intelligence, actively shaping the unfolding masterpiece that is your life.

From Character to Co-Author: The Profound Shift

Remember the old Laura King? The one who felt life was a pre-written script she had to follow? She's slowly fading away. Why? Because I've embraced the profound understanding that I am the co-author of my own story, partnering with God to write each chapter.

Think of your life as a collaborative novel. You're not just a character, nor are you the sole author. You're a co-writer, working in tandem with divine intelligence to craft a masterpiece. This perspective shift is like moving from black-and-white television to full-color, high-definition streaming. Suddenly, the world is vibrant with possibilities you never noticed before.

I remember the moment this truth hit me. I was staring at a blank page in my journal, feeling stuck and uninspired. Then it dawned on me—I was waiting for someone else to write my story. I was expecting life to dictate the plot, the characters, the outcomes. But the pen was in my hand all along. I just needed to start writing.

This realization is like discovering you have a magic pen. Not the kind that writes on its own, but one that, when you use it intentionally, seems to make the universe conspire to bring your words to life. It doesn't erase challenges or difficulties, but it does give you the power to reframe them, to see them as plot twists rather than dead ends.

> **Reflection Moment:** Think about a time when you felt like a passive character in your own life story versus a time when you actively shaped your narrative. How did these experiences differ in terms of your emotions, energy levels, and outcomes?

The Science of Co-Creation

While the concept of co-authoring your life might sound metaphorical, research in neuroscience and psychology reveals fascinating insights into how our brains literally construct our reality through the stories we tell ourselves. Studies in narrative psychology show that the way we frame our life experiences—the plots, themes, and roles we assign—dramatically impacts not just our emotional experience but our physiological responses and behavioral choices.[1]

What's particularly interesting is how our brain chemistry changes when we shift from a passive to an active relationship with our life narrative. When we view ourselves as victims of circumstance (passive characters), our bodies produce higher levels of stress hormones like cortisol.[2] However, when we adopt a co-authorship mindset, seeing ourselves as active partners in creating our reality, our brain chemistry shifts toward increased dopamine, serotonin, and endorphins—neurotransmitters associated with motivation, well-being, and resilience.[3]

Research in epigenetics—the study of how behaviors and environment can cause changes that affect the way your genes work—further supports this co-authorship model. Studies show that our thoughts, beliefs, and emotional states can literally turn genes on or off, influencing not just our mental experience but our physical health and biological functioning.[4] In a very real sense, the stories we tell ourselves and the meaning we assign to events can reshape our biological reality.

Now, just as every writer has their preferred tools and methods, you too can develop a toolkit for co-authoring your life. Here are some expanded techniques:

Character Development: Dive deep into self-reflection. What are your strengths? Your flaws? Your motivations? Just as a novelist might create a detailed character profile, create one for yourself. Then, intentionally put yourself in situations that will develop the traits you want to embody. If you want to be more courageous, deliberately face small fears. If you want to be more compassionate, seek out opportunities to help others.

World-Building: Your environment shapes your story. Curate your physical space to reflect the life you're writing. Surround yourself with objects, colors, and textures that inspire you. But go beyond the physical—shape your mental and emotional environment too. Choose media that uplifts you, relationships that support you, and practices that nourish your spirit.

Plot Twists: Life's unexpected turns are your co-author's contributions. Train yourself to ask, "how is this serving my story?" when faced with challenges. Perhaps a job loss is setting the stage for a career change you've been longing for. Maybe a relationship ending is making space for self-discovery. Learn to trust the plot, even when it seems to be going off course.

Pacing: Balance is key in any good story. Learn to recognize when you need to take bold action and when you need to pause for reflection. Create rituals for both—perhaps a morning routine for planning and an evening routine for reflecting. This rhythm will help you maintain momentum in your story without burning out.

Editing: Regular self-reflection is your editing process. Set aside time weekly or monthly to review your "draft." What's working well in your story? What needs revision? Be willing to let go of plotlines that no longer serve you, whether it's a job, a relationship, or a belief about yourself.

Collaboration: Cultivate your ability to recognize and act on universal cues. This might involve practicing mindfulness to stay present, learning to trust your intuition, or simply being open to unexpected opportunities. Divine intelligence often speaks in whispers—learn to listen closely.

FEATURED PRACTICE:
The Life Story Reframe

Use this powerful exercise to shift from passive character to active co-author:

1. **Identify a challenge**: Choose a current or past challenge that feels like something "happening to you." Write a brief paragraph describing this situation from the perspective of being a passive character in the story.

2. **Notice the language**: Circle all phrases that position you as a victim or passive recipient of circumstances (e.g., "This happened to me," "I had no choice," "I was forced to").

3. **Shift to co-authorship**: Rewrite the same situation, but this time position yourself as an active co-creator. Use phrases like "I chose," "I created," "I'm learning," "I'm using this to..." Even if you didn't choose the initial circumstance, you can choose your response and the meaning you assign.

4. **Find the purpose**: Add a sentence that begins with "This chapter in my story is serving me by..." and complete it authentically.

5. **Write the next scene**: Conclude with a paragraph beginning "And now I'm choosing to..." that describes how you'll actively shape the next part of this storyline.

Research in cognitive behavioral therapy shows that this type of narrative reframing significantly impacts not just our emotional response to challenges but our subsequent actions and outcomes.[5] By consciously shifting from victim language to creator language, we activate different neural pathways and literally change how our brains process the situation.

Daily Practices for the Co-Author

Now, let's look at how you can incorporate these techniques into your daily life. You probably don't want to try to do all of them, but pick one or two that resonate the most with you:

Morning Pages: Start each day by writing three pages of stream-of-consciousness thoughts. This practice, popularized by Julia Cameron, helps clear your mind and tap into your subconscious, where many of your story ideas originate.

Intention Setting: Before you start your day, set an intention for the chapter you're about to write. How do you want this day to contribute to your overall story?

Mindful Moments: Throughout the day, take brief pauses to check in with yourself. Are you actively co-creating, or have you slipped into passive mode? These moments of awareness can help you stay engaged in your story.

Evening Reflection: End each day by reflecting on the chapter you've just written. What were the key scenes? How did you develop as a character? What do you want to carry forward into tomorrow's writing?

Gratitude Practice: Regularly acknowledge the beauty in your story. This helps you maintain a positive perspective and attracts more positive plotlines.

Visualizations: Spend time visualizing future chapters of your story. This is like creating an outline for your novel—it gives you a direction to write towards.

Research in positive psychology suggests that people who engage in these types of intentional narrative practices report significantly higher levels of life satisfaction, purpose, and resilience than those who don't.[6] By consciously engaging with your life as a creative work-in-progress rather than a predetermined script, you activate what psychologists call your "narrative identity"—the evolving story that gives your life meaning and direction.[7]

Try This:

- Choose one daily practice from the list above and commit to it for two weeks
- Notice how this practice affects your sense of agency and authorship in your life
- Experiment with different practices to discover which ones most powerfully activate your co-author mindset

My Transformation: Living the Practices in Real Time

It's one thing to write about these principles and practices—it's another thing entirely to live them. As I've been writing this book over the past two years, I've been actively applying each chapter's teachings to my own life. The transformation has been profound, and I want to share some of this journey with you, not to boast but to show you that these principles aren't just theories—they're powerful tools for real-world transformation.

It began in 2023, when I received what I called my "triple threat diagnosis" in the introduction of this book: anxiety off the charts, chronic sleep disruption, and ADHD. That moment marked the beginning of what would become my most intense period of growth and transformation.

As I worked on each chapter of this book, I found myself living the very lessons I was writing about. I was creating a new life. Through the practices of self-love, authenticity, reprogramming limiting beliefs, and embracing infinite possibility, I began to write a new story for myself—one chapter at a time.

A pivotal moment came on October 9th, 2024—what my friend Mondo calls my "spiritual birthday." That day, I experienced a profound spiritual breakthrough. As I shared in an audio message to him:

"I am here to be an instrument for God and to allow His work to be done through me. And today I did quite a bit of healing work. I did a huge release of the shame I had been hanging on to from my seventh and eighth grade bullying experience, and forgave some key people in my life. I realized that prominent people in my life had put conditions on love. They did this without realizing it, so I must forgive them. I must forgive them for not seeing my gifts and my God-given potential."

That day, I took a bold step in co-authoring my story. For the first time, I created a LinkedIn post where I shared my faith boldly—something the old Laura would never have done for fear of professional judgment. The response was overwhelmingly positive. Not that external validation was the point, but it confirmed what I was feeling internally: I was finally in alignment. I was writing my authentic story without apology.

"I am congruent. I am authentic," I realized. "This note to myself is my reminder to stay grounded, to stay connected at all times, to ask what would God like me to know and what would God like me to do, and then be obedient to that."

Just twelve days later, on October 21st, another breakthrough came while I was at the North Shore with my husband's family. Looking around at my loved ones, I had a moment of crystal clarity, also in an audio message I recorded to myself:

"I realized why this is book so important to me. And yes, I am here to help so many people awaken to their truth by sharing my truth and my story."

But there was more.

In that moment at the North Shore I saw how much healing I had done in the past 18+ months—more than in my entire previous 41 years. I wasn't just processing my own trauma but the trauma of generations before me. I was transforming through the "renewing of my mind," moving from a place of brokenness and fear to one of wholeness and faith.

"Each chapter is the lesson I most needed to learn myself," I realized. "This is the advice my higher self has given to my human self. And I need to learn it and live it."

As I sat there with my family, I began to cry. Not because I was sad, but because I understood the reason for all the pain and heartache. I experienced a profound moment of presence that woke me up. I could see all the previous versions of myself from past years at the North Shore my 30-year-old self, my 31-year-old self, and so on—always rushing toward the future, always believing I would be "enough" someday, but never in the present moment.

"And I forgave her," I said through tears. "I forgave her for all the times she was rushing to the future...I was trying to be in the future and I'm like, oh my gosh, I got it. I got it. I really, really, really, really, really got it."

What I "got" was the profound beauty of being fully present, of shutting down the mind and ego to simply be in the perfectly made present moment with my family.

"I am perfect and whole without having to achieve and work and struggle and strive. I am enough in this moment."

This was the magnificent revelation I needed: that heaven exists in the present moment. That God speaks to us in the now. That true freedom comes not from rushing toward some future state of worthiness and enoughness but from embracing our inherent worthiness right here, right now.

"I see everything differently," I realized. "Everyone is a soul. Everyone's a spirit. And I just see the beauty in everyone and how it's all working out so perfectly. Even the messes are perfect."

This spiritual awakening began to manifest in my external reality. As I continued to apply the principles in this book, my professional life transformed dramatically. By December 2024, I was ready to have a courageous conversation that had been stirring in me for years: could I actually say out loud that I have a calling that I must explore? A calling that has been guiding me for years and years and years. Could I actually say out loud that a career in recruiting is not my entire future? Maybe it will play a role, but I am meant to share my gifts in other ways too? Could I actually say these things?

I walked into my boss's office, heart pounding. I was certain I was facing an either/or proposition: continue as I had been or leave to pursue this unknow "calling" practice full-time. What unfolded stunned me.

As I shared my conviction that I had a calling beyond recruiting, a calling that I had a hard time even verbalizing what it was. Was it coaching and workshops? Going back to school to pursue an advanced degree? Something in mental health? I just knew I had to be honest. Recruiting has been so good to me, and I want to honor the gift I have there, but my heart is leading me down a path of the unknown. I saw possibilities dawn in the eyes of my very shocked employer. Instead of the "choose one" ultimatum I expected, I heard "why not both?" In those 30 minutes, everything shifted.

I realized that the "impossible choice" I thought I was facing was actually a false dichotomy created by my own limiting beliefs. The conversation I'd been dreading became the doorway to a breakthrough. I could have had this conversation earlier, but I wasn't fully ready to stand in my truth and authentic power. Heck, I could have had it five years ago.

It all works out the way it's supposed to work out.

By January 2025, I had transitioned from full-time recruiting to a flexible arrangement where I spent half of my time recruiting and the other half devoted to coaching and providing in-person purpose workshops. My "side hustle" coaching practice exploded from just three clients to over nine in January alone. This became one of the most exciting periods of my life as I stepped into serving people in a way I had never allowed myself to before. And my learning amplified as I began teaching topics of this book, taking further steps toward self- mastery through repetition of these key concepts.

The financial abundance began flowing as well, but in a way I hadn't expected. For months prior to the December 2024 conversation, I had been praying for six months of income that would allow me to transition to "my calling" full-time. I was the breadwinner and I couldn't do anything to put my family in jeopardy. I'd probably prayed that prayer a hundred times, but always from a place of lack and separation—almost begging.

Then I decided to apply what I'd been writing about in this book. Instead of praying from lack, I began praying from gratitude and completion, as if what I desired was already done. I thanked God for the six months of income as if I had already received it, fully integrating that prayer into my body with genuine emotion.

The very next week, the money showed up from the most unexpected place.

This experience taught me the profound difference between asking from separation versus praying from oneness—between begging and genuinely thanking God in advance for what He's already done. It's all rooted in gratitude and knowing it is done.

I share these personal transformations not to impress you but to impress upon you the power of applied knowledge. There's a big difference between knowing and doing. I choose to do something with the wisdom I received through this book. I didn't just take it face value, I practiced. And practiced. And practiced some more. That is self-mastery. I am not special—I simply decided to pick up the pen and actively co-author my life with divine intelligence. And guess what, so can you.

The 4 A's Framework for Co-Authoring Your Life

To help you in this process of becoming a skilled co-author of your life, let's explore the Four A's of Co-Creation: Awareness, Attitude, Action, and Alignment.

1. Awareness: Read Your Current Chapter Carefully

Awareness is about reading your current chapter carefully. What themes are emerging? What patterns keep repeating? This isn't just about acknowledging where you are, but understanding how you got here and where this plot might be leading.

Research in narrative psychology shows that developing what scientists call "narrative intelligence"—the ability to recognize patterns and themes in your life story—significantly enhances your capacity to shape future chapters.[8] When you become aware of recurring plotlines in your story, you gain the power to consciously continue or revise them.

Try This:

- Identify three recurring themes or patterns in your current life chapter

- For each pattern, ask: "Is this a theme I want to continue developing, or is it time for a new direction?"
- Notice the "story language" you use when describing challenges or opportunities—does it position you as a victim, hero, or co-creator?

2. Attitude: Choose Your Story's Genre

Attitude is about choosing the genre of your story. Is it a tragedy or a hero's journey? A love story or an adventure? Your attitude colors every scene you write.

Research in cognitive psychology demonstrates that our expectations literally shape what we perceive and how we interpret events.[9] When you consciously choose the genre or emotional tone of your life story, you actually change how your brain processes and assigns meaning to your experiences.

Try This:

- Identify the current "genre" of your life story—is it a drama, comedy, adventure, mystery?
- Experiment with deliberately shifting to a different genre for a week
- Notice how this shift in attitude changes both your perception and your actions

3. Action: Put Pen to Paper

Action is where you put pen to paper. It's not enough to imagine your story; you must write it into existence. Every choice, every word, every gesture is a sentence in your ongoing narrative.

Studies in behavioral psychology show that taking action, even small steps, creates what scientists call a "virtuous cycle" of increased confidence and further action.[10] Each deliberate choice you make as the co-author of your story strengthens your author identity and makes further authorship easier.

Try This:

- Identify one area of your life where you've been passive and choose one small, active step
- Practice "story-based decision-making" by asking "What would make the best story?" when facing choices
- Create daily or weekly writing rituals that help you actively engage with your life narrative

4. Alignment: Ensure Your Story Resonates with Your Core Values

Alignment is about ensuring your story resonates with your core values and the universal laws. It's like finding the perfect rhythm in your writing, where everything flows seamlessly.

Research in positive psychology has identified "narrative coherence"—the sense that one's life story has consistency, purpose, and meaning—as a key factor in psychological well-being.[11] When your daily choices and overall life direction align with your deepest values and sense of purpose, you experience this coherence as a profound sense of rightness and flow.

Try This:

- Identify your 3-5 core values and assess how well your current story honors them
- Notice moments of "story dissonance"—when your actions conflict with your authentic narrative
- Create a personal mission statement that captures the essence of the story you're co-authoring

When you embrace these elements, you begin to write a life story that's uniquely yours, yet universally inspiring. You're not just existing in a pre-written script; you're actively co-creating a masterpiece with the universe.

So, what story will you write? Will it be a tale of transformation, of love, of adventure? Will it inspire, challenge, or comfort? The choice is yours. The pen is in your hand, the universe is your co-author, and the blank page of possibility awaits.

Start writing your masterpiece. Don't worry about perfect prose; life is often messy and beautiful in its imperfection. Write boldly, write authentically, write with the knowledge that your story has the power to change not just your world, but the world of those around you.

As I've experienced in my own journey—from always-on anxiety, sleep disruption, and ADHD to a life of authentic alignment, spiritual connection, and purposeful work—the transformation can be profound when you pick up the pen. The shift from being a passive character to an active co-author changes everything.

And remember, you're not writing alone. Divine intelligence, God, the Universe—whatever name resonates with you—is your co-author, working alongside you, guiding your hand when you listen for the whispers, suggesting plot twists that serve your highest development, introducing characters who help you grow.

Your story matters. Your voice matters. Your unique way of co-creating with the divine matters. The world needs your story—not someone else's, not some edited version you think will be more acceptable—but the raw, real, authentic masterpiece that only you and your divine co-author can write together.

So pick up your pen. Turn the page. And begin.

Key Takeaways:

- You are not a passive character in a predetermined script but an active co-author working with divine intelligence
- The way you frame your life experiences literally changes your brain chemistry and biological functioning
- Writers' tools like character development, world-building, and editing can be applied to consciously craft your life story
- Daily narrative practices like intention setting and evening reflection strengthen your co-author mindset

- Transformation begins when you shift from viewing challenges as things "happening to you" to seeing them as purposeful plot developments
- Praying from completion and gratitude rather than lack creates powerful shifts in both inner and outer reality
- The present moment is where you access your co-author's wisdom—not in regrets about the past or worries about the future
- Your unique story, authentically lived and shared, creates ripples of possibility for others

Expert Insights on Co-Creating Your Life Story

"Life isn't about finding yourself. Life is about creating yourself." — George Bernard Shaw, whose dramatic works and personal philosophy emphasized human agency and creative self-determination.[12]

"We do not write in order to be understood; we write in order to understand." — C.S. Lewis, whose literary works explored the relationship between human choice and divine guidance.[13]

"The universe is made of stories, not of atoms." — Muriel Rukeyser, whose poetry and activism demonstrated the power of narrative to shape both personal and collective reality.[14]

"Don't ask what the world needs. Ask what makes you come alive, and go do it. Because what the world needs is people who have come alive." — Howard Thurman, whose theological work emphasized the co-creative relationship between human purpose and divine intelligence.[15]

Your Turn: Reflective Free Writing

Take a few minutes now to begin consciously co-authoring your life story. Find a quiet space, set a timer for 10 minutes, and write continuously without editing or judging what comes up. You might consider these prompts:

Free Writing Prompts:

- If your life were a book, what would the title of your current chapter be? What's the main theme or lesson?
- What plot twist or character development are you ready to write into your story?
- Where have you been a passive character in your story, and how might you reclaim your co-author role?
- If you could collaborate with divine intelligence to create any life story, what would the next chapter look like?
- What limiting narrative have you been telling yourself that you're ready to revise or release?

Unlocking Your Inner Light to Shine Brighter

A s we come to the end of this journey, I want to remind you of a fundamental truth: you are here for a reason. You are not a random accident or a cosmic coincidence. You are a deliberate creation, a being of light and love, born with a specific mission to fulfill.

We each come into this world with something special that only we can provide. Our goal in this lifetime is not to conform and follow the standards of the external world, but to discover who we really are and become that. Your creative talent and expression are your gifts to the world. It's not selfish to go on a quest to discover the very best of who you are. It's your responsibility to share the very best of who you are.

The Difference Between Knowing and Doing

As you reflect on these tools and takeaways, I want to emphasize something crucial: there's a profound difference between knowing and doing. We all know we should eat better, but do we? We know we should exercise regularly, but do we follow through? Knowledge without implementation creates little change.

This book contains dozens of transformative tools and practices. But they won't change your life sitting on these pages. The magic happens when you apply them—consistently, courageously, imperfectly.

If you haven't already, make sure you download and print out the special bonus I made for you: www.lauraeking.com/bonus

This allows you to have all the practices from the book in one compact location with extra room for your notes and reflection.

I invite you to choose just one tool from this summary that resonates most deeply with you right now. Commit to practicing it daily for the next 21 days. Don't try to implement everything at once—that's a recipe for overwhelm and abandonment. Start small, build momentum, and watch how this single practice begins rippling through other areas of your life.

Then, when you've integrated this tool into your life, choose another. And another. Layer these practices gradually, allowing each one to take root before adding more. This isn't a race—it's a lifelong journey of unveiling your light.

And when you experience the transformation these practices create, please share this book with someone you love. Gift them not just the pages but your testimony—your real-life experience of how these principles changed you. Let's start a ripple effect of all of us shining as brightly as we can.

Let's Keep In Touch

I am beyond excited to see how your life transforms as you implement these practices. Your journey of unlocking your inner light matters deeply to me, and I'd love to support you further.

> If you enjoyed this book, you'll love my Friday newsletter. Join my email list at www.lauraeking.com, or follow me on Instagram (@_lauraeking) and LinkedIn for the latest updates.

As I write this, I sense that my own path is evolving—moving from primarily one-on-one coaching to models that allow me to support more people in their awakening journeys. It will be beautiful to see how God orchestrates this shift. Because I know that it's not me—it's in my full surrender that the most magnificent things will be done through me. I am simply a channel for God to do what only God can do.

If you feel called to additional support on your journey, I invite you visit my website for programs and trainings designed to deepen your transformation.

I am grateful beyond words for this life, blessed to be alive in this transformative time, and incredibly excited to hear how this book has impacted your journey. However our paths may intersect from here, know that I am cheering for you, believing in your light, and holding space for your brightest expression to emerge.

A Prayer for Your Journey

As you close these pages and continue writing your unique story, I offer this prayer:

Divine God, Creator of the Most High, Source of all light and love,

I ask your blessing upon the precious soul holding this book. May they recognize the divine spark within them that has always been there, waiting to be fully expressed. Grant them the courage to shed what no longer serves, the wisdom to embrace their authentic truth, and the love to see themselves through your eyes.

Walk beside them as they implement these practices. When doubt arises, remind them of their infinite potential. When fear emerges, fill them with your perfect love that casts out all fear. When old patterns resurface, guide them back to awareness and conscious choice.

May every person who has journeyed through these pages become a beacon of light in this world. May their transformation create ripples that touch countless others. May they remember that they are never alone—that your divine presence flows through them, guiding every step when they surrender and listen.

Thank you for the privilege of connection, for the miracle of growth, and for the beautiful unfolding of each unique soul's purpose. May we all shine brighter, individually and collectively, illuminating this world with the light of truth, joy, and love.

Amen.

So shine on, my friend. Shine brightly, shine boldly, shine unapologetically.

The world is waiting for your light.

With love and deep belief in your magnificence,

Laura

References

Chapter 1:

[1]Brown, B. (2012). Daring Greatly: How the Courage to Be Vulnerable Transforms the Way We Live, Love, Parent, and Lead. Gotham Books.

[2]Brewer, J. A., Worhunsky, P. D., Gray, J. R., Tang, Y. Y., Weber, J., & Kober, H. (2011). Meditation experience is associated with differences in default mode network activity and connectivity. Proceedings of the National Academy of Sciences, 108(50), 20254-20259.

[3]Dweck, C. S. (2006). Mindset: The New Psychology of Success. Random House.

[4]Dyer, W. W. (2009). Excuses Begone!: How to Change Lifelong, Self-Defeating Thinking Habits. Hay House.

[5]Watterson, B. (1990). Some Thoughts on the Real World by One Who Glimpsed It and Fled. Kenyon College Commencement Speech.

[6]Tolle, E. (2004). The Power of Now: A Guide to Spiritual Enlightenment. New World Library.

[7]Maraboli, S. (2013). Unapologetically You: Reflections on Life and the Human Experience. Better Today Publishing.

[8]Eger, E. (2017). The Choice: Embrace the Possible. Scribner.

Chapter 2:

[1]Neff, K. D., & Germer, C. K. (2018). The Mindful Self-Compassion Workbook. Guilford Press.

[2]Brown, B. (2010). The Gifts of Imperfection: Let Go of Who You Think You're Supposed to Be and Embrace Who You Are. Hazelden Publishing.

[3]Neff, K. D., & Vonk, R. (2009). Self-compassion versus global self-esteem: Two different ways of relating to oneself. Journal of Personality, 77, 23-50.

[4]Jung, C. G. (1969). The archetypes and the collective unconscious (2nd ed.). Princeton University Press.

Chapter 3:

[1]Davidson, R. J., & Begley, S. (2012). The Emotional Life of Your Brain: How Its Unique Patterns Affect the Way You Think, Feel, and Live—and How You Can Change Them. Hudson Street Press.

[2]Hammond, D. C. (2011). What is neurofeedback: An update. Journal of Neurotherapy, 15(4), 305-336.

[3]Davidson, R. J., & Lutz, A. (2008). Buddha's brain: Neuroplasticity and meditation. IEEE Signal Processing Magazine, 25(1), 176-174.

[4]Fredrickson, B. L. (2009). Positivity: Groundbreaking Research Reveals How to Embrace the Hidden Strength of Positive Emotions, Overcome Negativity, and Thrive. Crown Publishing Group.

[5]Burchard, B. (2017). High Performance Habits: How Extraordinary People Become That Way. Hay House.

[6]Csikszentmihalyi, M. (2008). Flow: The Psychology of Optimal Experience. Harper Perennial Modern Classics.

[7]Hanson, R. (2013). Hardwiring Happiness: The New Brain Science of Contentment, Calm, and Confidence. Harmony Books.

[8]Christensen, J. F., & Calvo-Merino, B. (2013). Dance as a subject for empirical aesthetics. Psychology of Aesthetics, Creativity, and the Arts, 7(1), 76-88.

[9]Jobs, S. (2005). Stanford University Commencement Address.

[10]Nouwen, H. J. M. (2002). Here and Now: Living in the Spirit. Crossroad Publishing Company.

[11]Tolle, E. (2004). The Power of Now: A Guide to Spiritual Enlightenment. New World Library.

[12]Burchard, B. (2014). The Motivation Manifesto: 9 Declarations to Claim Your Personal Power. Hay House.

Chapter 4:

[1]Biswas-Diener, R., Kashdan, T. B., & Minhas, G. (2011). A dynamic approach to psychological strength development and intervention. The Journal of Positive Psychology, 6(2), 106-118.

[2]Seligman, M. E. P. (2002). Authentic Happiness: Using the New Positive Psychology to Realize Your Potential for Lasting Fulfillment. Free Press.

[3]Niemiec, R. M. (2018). Character Strengths Interventions: A Field Guide for Practitioners. Hogrefe Publishing.

[4]Kotler, S. (2014). The Rise of Superman: Decoding the Science of Ultimate Human Performance. New Harvest.

[5]Rath, T. (2007). StrengthsFinder 2.0. Gallup Press.

[6]Cuddy, A. (2015). Presence: Bringing Your Boldest Self to Your Biggest Challenges. Little, Brown and Company.

[7]Csikszentmihalyi, M. (2008). Flow: The Psychology of Optimal Experience. Harper Perennial Modern Classics.

[8]Wrzesniewski, A., McCauley, C., Rozin, P., & Schwartz, B. (1997). Jobs, careers, and callings: People's relations to their work. Journal of Research in Personality, 31(1), 21-33.

[9]Attributed to Albert Einstein, though the exact source is unconfirmed.

[10]Buscaglia, L. (1986). Living, Loving and Learning. Fawcett Books.

[11]Franklin, B. (1758). Poor Richard's Almanack.

[12]Campbell, J. (1991). The Power of Myth. Anchor Books.

Chapter 5:

[1]Eisenberger, N. I., Lieberman, M. D., & Williams, K. D. (2003). Does rejection hurt? An fMRI study of social exclusion. Science, 302(5643), 290-292.

[2]Vogel, E. A., Rose, J. P., Roberts, L. R., & Eckles, K. (2014). Social comparison, social media, and self-esteem. Psychology of Popular Media Culture, 3(4), 206-222.

[3]Neff, K. D., & Germer, C. K. (2013). A pilot study and randomized controlled trial of the mindful self-compassion program. Journal of Clinical Psychology, 69(1), 28-44.

[4]Festinger, L. (1954). A theory of social comparison processes. Human Relations, 7(2), 117-140.

[5]Wheeler, L., & Miyake, K. (1992). Social comparison in everyday life. Journal of Personality and Social Psychology, 62(5), 760-773.

[6]Ryan, R. M., & Deci, E. L. (2000). Self-determination theory and the facilitation of intrinsic motivation, social development, and well-being. American Psychologist, 55(1), 68-78.

[7]Farb, N. A. S., Segal, Z. V., Mayberg, H., Bean, J., McKeon, D., Fatima, Z., & Anderson, A. K. (2007). Attending to the present: Mindfulness meditation reveals distinct neural modes of self-reference. Social Cognitive and Affective Neuroscience, 2(4), 313-322.

[8]Neff, K. D. (2011). Self-compassion, self-esteem, and well-being. Social and Personality Psychology Compass, 5(1), 1-12.

[9]Gilbert, P., & Procter, S. (2006). Compassionate mind training for people with high shame and self-criticism: Overview and pilot study of a group therapy approach. Clinical Psychology & Psychotherapy, 13(6), 353-379.

[10]Hunt, M. G., Marx, R., Lipson, C., & Young, J. (2018). No more FOMO: Limiting social media decreases loneliness and depression. Journal of Social and Clinical Psychology, 37(10), 751-768.

[11]Sheldon, K. M., & Kasser, T. (1998). Pursuing personal goals: Skills enable progress, but not all progress is beneficial. Personality and Social Psychology Bulletin, 24(12), 1319-1331.

[13]Furtick, S. (2014). Crash the Chatterbox: Hearing God's Voice Above All Others. Multnomah Books.

[14]Brown, B. (2010). The Gifts of Imperfection: Let Go of Who You Think You're Supposed to Be and Embrace Who You Are. Hazelden Publishing.

[15]Campbell, J. (1991). The Power of Myth. Anchor Books.

Chapter 6:

[1]Kinomura, S., Larsson, J., Gulyás, B., & Roland, P. E. (1996). Activation by attention of the human reticular formation and thalamic intralaminar nuclei. Science, 271(5248), 512-515.

[2]Mohr, D. C., & Pelletier, D. (2006). A temporal framework for understanding the effects of stressful life events on inflammation in patients with multiple sclerosis. Brain, Behavior, and Immunity, 20(1), 27-36.

[3]Pennebaker, J. W. (1997). Writing about emotional experiences as a therapeutic process. Psychological Science, 8(3), 162-166.

[4]Dispenza, J. (2017). Becoming Supernatural: How Common People Are Doing the Uncommon. Hay House, Inc.

[5]Klontz, B., Britt, S. L., Mentzer, J., & Klontz, T. (2011). Money beliefs and financial behaviors: Development of the Klontz Money Script Inventory. Journal of Financial Therapy, 2(1), 1-22.

[6]Kosslyn, S. M., Ganis, G., & Thompson, W. L. (2001). Neural foundations of imagery. Nature Reviews Neuroscience, 2(9), 635-642.

[7]Dweck, C. S. (2006). Mindset: The New Psychology of Success. Random House.

[8]Gcndlin, E. T. (1981). Focusing. Bantam Books.

[9]Bandura, A. (1977). Self-efficacy: Toward a unifying theory of behavioral change. Psychological Review, 84(2), 191-215.

[10]Ryan, R. M., & Deci, E. L. (2000). Self-determination theory and the facilitation of intrinsic motivation, social development, and well-being. American Psychologist, 55(1), 68-78.

[11]Dyer, W. W. (2004). The Power of Intention: Learning to Co-create Your World Your Way. Hay House.

[12]Planck, M. (1944). Das Wesen der Materie [The Nature of Matter], speech at Florence, Italy.

[13]Dispenza, J. (2012). Breaking the Habit of Being Yourself: How to Lose Your Mind and Create a New One. Hay House.

[14]Lincoln, A. (attributed).

Chapter 7:

[1]Simons, T. (2002). Behavioral integrity: The perceived alignment between managers' words and deeds as a research focus. Organization Science, 13(1), 18-35.

[2]Otake, K., Shimai, S., Tanaka-Matsumi, J., Otsui, K., & Fredrickson, B. L. (2006). Happy people become happier through kindness: A counting kindnesses intervention. Journal of Happiness Studies, 7(3), 361-375.

[3]Zak, P. J., & Barraza, J. A. (2013). The neurobiology of collective action. Frontiers in Neuroscience, 7, 211.

[4]Gottman, J. M., & Silver, N. (2015). The Seven Principles for Making Marriage Work. Harmony Books.

[5]Harter, J. K., Schmidt, F. L., & Agrawal, S. (2009). Q12 Meta-Analysis: The Relationship Between Engagement at Work and Organizational Outcomes. Gallup.

[6]Grant, A. M., & Dutton, J. E. (2012). Beneficiary or benefactor: Are people more prosocial when they reflect on receiving or giving? Psychological Science, 23(9), 1033-1039.

[7]Niemiec, R. M. (2018). Character Strengths Interventions: A Field Guide for Practitioners. Hogrefe Publishing.

[8]Stokoe, E. (2018). Talk: The Science of Conversation. Little, Brown Book Group.

[9]Nickerson, R. S. (1998). Confirmation bias: A ubiquitous phenomenon in many guises. Review of General Psychology, 2(2), 175-220.

[10]Gollwitzer, P. M., & Sheeran, P. (2006). Implementation intentions and goal achievement: A meta-analysis of effects and processes. Advances in Experimental Social Psychology, 38, 69-119.

[11]Brown, B. (2018). Dare to Lead: Brave Work. Tough Conversations. Whole Hearts. Random House.

[12]Mead, M. (1928/2001). Coming of Age in Samoa. Harper Perennial.

[13]Angelou, M. (1994). The Complete Collected Poems of Maya Angelou. Random House.

[14]James, W. (1890/1950). The Principles of Psychology. Dover Publications.

[15]Gandhi, M. K. (1948). Non-violence in Peace and War. Navajivan Publishing House.

Chapter 8:

[1]Wood, A. M., Linley, P. A., Maltby, J., Baliousis, M., & Joseph, S. (2008). The authentic personality: A theoretical and empirical conceptualization and the development of the Authenticity Scale. Journal of Counseling Psychology, 55(3), 385-399.

[2]Edmondson, A. C. (1999). Psychological safety and learning behavior in work teams. Administrative Science Quarterly, 44(2), 350-383.

[3]Pennebaker, J. W. (2018). Expressive writing in psychological science. Perspectives on Psychological Science, 13(2), 226-229.

[4]David, S. (2016). Emotional Agility: Get Unstuck, Embrace Change, and Thrive in Work and Life. Penguin.

[5]Kernis, M. H., & Goldman, B. M. (2006). A multicomponent conceptualization of authenticity: Theory and research. Advances in Experimental Social Psychology, 38, 283-357.

[6]Leroy, H., Anseel, F., Dimitrova, N. G., & Sels, L. (2013). Mindfulness, authentic functioning, and work engagement: A growth modeling approach. Journal of Vocational Behavior, 82(3), 238-247.

[7]Avolio, B. J., & Gardner, W. L. (2005). Authentic leadership development: Getting to the root of positive forms of leadership. The Leadership Quarterly, 16(3), 315-338.

[8]Neff, K. D., & Dahm, K. A. (2015). Self-compassion: What it is, what it does, and how it relates to mindfulness. In Handbook of mindfulness and self-regulation (pp. 121-137). Springer.

[9]Farb, N. A., Segal, Z. V., Mayberg, H., Bean, J., McKeon, D., Fatima, Z., & Anderson, A. K. (2007). Attending to the present: mindfulness meditation reveals distinct neural modes of self-reference. Social Cognitive and Affective Neuroscience, 2(4), 313-322.

[10]Ryff, C. D. (1989). Happiness is everything, or is it? Explorations on the meaning of psychological well-being. Journal of Personality and Social Psychology, 57(6), 1069-1081.

[11]Rogers, C. R. (1961). On becoming a person: A therapist's view of psychotherapy. Houghton Mifflin.

[12]Sheldon, K. M., & Kasser, T. (2001). Getting older, getting better? Personal strivings and psychological maturity across the life span. Developmental Psychology, 37(4), 491-501.

[13]Brown, B. (2010). The Gifts of Imperfection: Let Go of Who You Think You're Supposed to Be and Embrace Who You Are. Hazelden Publishing.

[14]Rumi, J. (13th century). The Essential Rumi, translated by Coleman Barks (1995). Harper Collins.

[15]Plato (399 BCE). Apology. Hackett Publishing Company.

[16]Emerson, R. W. (1841). Self-Reliance. Essays: First Series.

Chapter 9:

[1]Doidge, N. (2007). The Brain That Changes Itself: Stories of Personal Triumph from the Frontiers of Brain Science. Penguin Books.

[2]Schwartz, J. M., & Begley, S. (2002). The Mind and the Brain: Neuroplasticity and the Power of Mental Force. Regan Books.

[3]Merzenich, M. M. (2013). Soft-Wired: How the New Science of Brain Plasticity Can Change Your Life. Parnassus Publishing.

[4]Hanson, R. (2013). Hardwiring Happiness: The New Brain Science of Contentment, Calm, and Confidence. Harmony Books.

[5]Seligman, M. E. P. (2011). Flourish: A Visionary New Understanding of Happiness and Well-being. Free Press.

[6]Siegel, D. J. (2007). The Mindful Brain: Reflection and Attunement in the Cultivation of Well-Being. W. W. Norton & Company.

[7]Kashdan, T. B., & Silvia, P. J. (2009). Curiosity and interest: The benefits of thriving on novelty and challenge. In S. J. Lopez & C. R. Snyder (Eds.), Oxford handbook of positive psychology (pp. 367–374). Oxford University Press.

[8]Lally, P., van Jaarsveld, C. H. M., Potts, H. W. W., & Wardle, J. (2010). How are habits formed: Modelling habit formation in the real world. European Journal of Social Psychology, 40(6), 998-1009.

[9]Sheldon, K. M., & Elliot, A. J. (1999). Goal striving, need satisfaction, and longitudinal well-being: The self-concordance model. Journal of Personality and Social Psychology, 76(3), 482-497.

[10]Davidson, R. J., & Begley, S. (2012). The Emotional Life of Your Brain: How Its Unique Patterns Affect the Way You Think, Feel, and Live—and How You Can Change Them. Hudson Street Press.

[11]Merzenich, M. M. (2013). Soft-Wired: How the New Science of Brain Plasticity Can Change Your Life. Parnassus Publishing.

[12]Frankl, V. E. (1959/2006). Man's Search for Meaning. Beacon Press.

[13]Gandhi, M. K. (1948). Non-violence in Peace and War. Navajivan Publishing House.

[14]Rogers, C. R. (1961). On Becoming a Person: A Therapist's View of Psychotherapy. Houghton Mifflin.

Chapter 10:

[1]Seligman, M. E. P. (2011). Flourish: A Visionary New Understanding of Happiness and Well-being. Free Press.

[2]Eagleman, D. (2011). Incognito: The Secret Lives of the Brain. Pantheon Books.

[3]Branden, N. (1994). The Six Pillars of Self-Esteem. Bantam Books.

[4]Christakis, N. A., & Fowler, J. H. (2009). Connected: The Surprising Power of Our Social Networks and How They Shape Our Lives. Little, Brown and Company.

[5]Southwick, S. M., & Charney, D. S. (2018). Resilience: The Science of Mastering Life's Greatest Challenges. Cambridge University Press.

[6]Crum, A. J., Salovey, P., & Achor, S. (2013). Rethinking stress: The role of mindsets in determining the stress response. Journal of Personality and Social Psychology, 104(4), 716-733.

[7]Jamieson, J. P., Nock, M. K., & Mendes, W. B. (2012). Mind over matter: Reappraising arousal improves cardiovascular and cognitive responses to stress. Journal of Experimental Psychology: General, 141(3), 417-422.

[8]Balcetis, E., & Dunning, D. (2006). See what you want to see: Motivational influences on visual perception. Journal of Personality and Social Psychology, 91(4), 612-625.

[9]Bar, M. (2009). The proactive brain: Memory for predictions. Philosophical Transactions of the Royal Society B: Biological Sciences, 364(1521), 1235-1243.

[10]Bandura, A. (1997). Self-efficacy: The Exercise of Control. W.H. Freeman and Company.

[11]McCraty, R., & Zayas, M. A. (2014). Cardiac coherence, self-regulation, autonomic stability, and psychosocial well-being. Frontiers in Psychology, 5, 1090.

[12]Dyer, W. W. (2004). The Power of Intention: Learning to Co-create Your World Your Way. Hay House.

[13]Chopra, D. (1994). The Seven Spiritual Laws of Success: A Practical Guide to the Fulfillment of Your Dreams. Amber-Allen Publishing.

[14]King, M. L., Jr. (1963). Strength to Love. Harper & Row.

[15]Roosevelt, E. (1960). You Learn by Living: Eleven Keys for a More Fulfilling Life. Harper & Brothers.

Chapter 11:

[1]Brown, B. (2010). The Gifts of Imperfection: Let Go of Who You Think You're Supposed to Be and Embrace Who You Are. Hazelden Publishing.

[2]Rumi, J. (13th century). The Essential Rumi, translated by Coleman Barks (1995). Harper Collins.

[3]Chopra, D. (2015). The Soul of Leadership: Unlocking Your Potential for Greatness. Harmony Books.

Chapter 12:

[1]McAdams, D. P. (2001). The psychology of life stories. Review of General Psychology, 5(2), 100-122.

[2]Pennebaker, J. W., & Seagal, J. D. (1999). Forming a story: The health benefits of narrative. Journal of Clinical Psychology, 55(10), 1243-1254.

[3]Newberg, A. B., & Waldman, M. R. (2012). Words Can Change Your Brain: 12 Conversation Strategies to Build Trust, Resolve Conflict, and Increase Intimacy. Penguin.

[4]Church, D. (2009). The Genie in Your Genes: Epigenetic Medicine and the New Biology of Intention. Energy Psychology Press.

[5]White, M., & Epston, D. (1990). Narrative Means to Therapeutic Ends. W. W. Norton & Company.

[6]Seligman, M. E. P. (2011). Flourish: A Visionary New Understanding of Happiness and Well-being. Free Press.

[7]Singer, J. A. (2004). Narrative identity and meaning making across the adult lifespan: An introduction. Journal of Personality, 72(3), 437-460.

[8]Randall, W. L. (1999). Narrative intelligence and the novelty of our lives. Journal of Aging Studies, 13(1), 11-28.

[9]Langer, E. J. (2009). Counterclockwise: Mindful Health and the Power of Possibility. Ballantine Books.

[10]Bandura, A. (1997). Self-efficacy: The Exercise of Control. W.H. Freeman and Company.

[11]Bauer, J. J., McAdams, D. P., & Pals, J. L. (2008). Narrative identity and eudaimonic well-being. Journal of Happiness Studies, 9(1), 81-104.

[12]Shaw, G. B. (1903). Man and Superman. Constable and Company Limited.

[13]Lewis, C. S. (1956). Till We Have Faces: A Myth Retold. Harcourt Brace & Company.

[14]Rukeyser, M. (1968). The Speed of Darkness. Random House.

[15]Thurman, H. (1953). Meditations of the Heart. Harper & Brothers.

About the Author

Laura King is a transformation guide for high achievers ready to lead with both impact and inner peace. With over 30,000 interviews under her belt as an executive recruiter, Laura has seen firsthand what most success stories leave out—the burnout, the imposter syndrome, the quiet question: *Is this really it?* Her work reveals a powerful truth: the highest-performing leaders aren't the ones hustling hardest—they're the ones most aligned with who they truly are.

Laura lives in Minnesota with her husband and their four children. A lifelong wellness enthusiast, she believes in moving energy through both mindset and movement. Deeply rooted in her community, Laura brings that same heart-forward presence to her local circles as she does to national audiences. Through speaking, coaching and transformational workshops, her mission remains the same: to help people rise—not by striving harder, but by stepping fully into their peak, their soul-aligned self.

www.lauraeking.com